HEALING FOR THE MILLIONS

The Amazing Dynamind Technique

by Serge

First English Edition 2004
ISBN #1-890850-20-9

Published by
Hunaworks
P.O. Box 223009
Princeville HI 96722

Dedication

This book is gratefully dedicated to the hundreds of clients and subjects whose personal experiences with the Dynamind Technique formed the major part of its content.

Acknowledgements

I wish to acknowledge most of all those whose deep interest and faith in the Dynamind Technique induced them to become Practitioners and Teachers, and who thereby made this book possible by their inspiration and dedication to helping others to help themselves.

In addition, I want to express great appreciation to my proofreader, Peggy Kemp, and to my ever-willing, primary test subject, Gloria King.

TABLE OF CONTENTS

INTRODUCTION

The world is in trouble and it needs healing badly. Ecological disasters, economic woes, political turmoil, wars and battles and skirmishes, disease epidemics, and social unrest or despair ... none of this is new, even though it constantly feeds the news. If we want to have any hope of changing the situation, however, we must answer two questions: Why is it happening? And, is there anything that we can we do about it?

I think I have answers to both of those questions. Not the ONLY answers, of course, because there are many paths to anywhere we want to go. But I do think I have answers that are useful.

The world needs healing because people need healing. We cannot heal the world, because "the world" is nothing but an abstract concept used to represent all the billions of people and other things that make up the world. We cannot heal society for the same reason, nor can we heal a government, which is nothing more than a general name we give to a lot of individual people working within a more or less organized abstract structure. We cannot even heal diseases, as experience shows. Our "wars" on cancer, heart disease, diabetes, and such non-disease illnesses as drug and alcohol addiction, and obesity, have not been successful except in cases where individual people have recovered.

Many ecological disasters happen because individual people selfishly decide to do things that adversely affect the environment. Economic woes occur because individual

1

greedy or fearful people act in ways that bring that about. Political turmoil and the wars, battles, and skirmishes that often accompany them, are brought about by individual people who are angry and afraid. Disease epidemics, in my opinion, spread out when a sufficient number of individual people have lost touch with their bodies and their feelings. And social unrest or despair comes from individual people who feel helpless or depressed.

What we most definitely can do is to heal, or at least facilitate the healing, of individual people. What difference will that make, you may ask? How will the healing of individual people result in changing all the things that I discussed above?

Well, I have a theory. It goes like this: the better people feel physically and emotionally, the more clear their thinking will be, and the better their decisions will be for the community as a whole. And conversely, the more clear their thinking is, the better they will feel physically and emotionally and the more they will tend to behave in ways that are more in harmony with their social and physical environment. I've tested this theory in small group situations over many years in a number of different countries, and the results have been so encouraging that I would like to see it tried on a much larger scale.

More simply put, we can change the world by changing people, or better, by giving people the tools to change themselves.

The changing of the world will not be done by advertising, no matter how extensive or well-designed. It will not be done by excessively expensive projects and processes, nor by bigger and better weapons either actual or metaphorical. It will never be done by trying to heal abstract concepts that only represent people. It can only be done by healing individual people one at a time, or by helping them to heal themselves.

Fortunately, there are millions of people in various healing professions working every day to heal individual people around the world. Unfortunately, there are many millions more who are not being healed, or who are not being healed effectively. And those millions of healers working one on one, for all their good work, are extremely inefficient in terms of time and cost for the purpose of expanding their services.

If only there were a way to heal more people more effectively and at very little expense. Actually, there is. To be truthful, there are probably many, many ways, but I am going to present you with one. It's called "The Dynamind Technique," and this book is about how to use it. Its advantages are that it is designed for people to use it on themselves, but it can also be done by one person for someone else; it can be used for any physical, emotional, mental or situational problem; it can be used alone or in combination with any other treatment or process; it is so simple that a three-year-old can learn it after a one-minute demonstration.

As for cost-effectiveness, it's free. A basic manual on The Dynamind Technique, or DMT as we often call it, is available in many languages as a free download through the website www.alohainternational.org, or as a single booklet in English from Aloha International, PO Box 223009, Princeville HI 96722 USA. Eventually, we hope to have it made available in every language in the world.

This book, however, is not free, because it is an in-depth look at the structure and application of DMT. Like many simple things, Dynamind has many levels of potential mastery. This book can be thought of as a kind of prelude to mastery of the technique for those who want to explore all of its possibilities, and as a more professional guide for those who want to teach it from a position of greater background knowledge. It is also for those who just want to know more about how to heal the world.

The Birthing

The Dynamind Technique was born in March of the year 2000. Of course, there was a decent period of conception and embryonic development long before that, but it didn't become a visible, viable technique until its actual birth in that month.

I have been actively involved in learning healing strategies since the age of fourteen, when my father began teaching me isometric exercises, self hypnosis and telepathic communication. Since then I have been engaged in an ongoing search for efficient methods of inducing positive change in mind, body and circumstances, especially in the areas of hypnosis, acupressure, breathing techniques and guided imagery.

As a clinical hypnotherapist for ten years I did considerable experimentation with the power of words, concluding that the "state of hypnosis" was really a state of more or less intensive focus induced by words that evoked certain responses in the subject. I found that anyone could be hypnotized in seconds if you used words that captured their attention. I also experimented with symbols, physical touch and energy fields during the same period and found that each of these could produce the same "hypnotic state." Additionally, all four of these methods could activate a process of change in the subject, although at the time I did not understand exactly how. I also used imaginary "intensity scales" for emotional feelings and physical sensations. I quickly discovered that it had nothing to do with my power as a hypnotist, but rather with the power which the subject invested in the process, the technique itself, and to some extent, my perceived role or my charisma. Additional verbal techniques I studied were affirmations, directions, blessings, suggestive therapy, and Lozanov's Suggestology.

I began my work with acupressure by studying about acupuncture while obtaining a degree in Asian Studies at the University of Colorado. Over the years I became proficient at Shiatsu, Do-In, and a system called "Self Therap-Ease." I also studied and practiced Reflexology, which demonstrated to me that the Chinese meridian system was a cultural concept and not a physiological one. It was clear, however, that the points were physiological and that they became sore under stress. I learned that the soreness at these points could be relieved by acupuncture (which I have experienced, but never practiced), heat, electrical stimulation, pressure, massage, tapping and imagination. The system of Kahi Loa that I learned from Laka, my *hanai* Hawaiian aunt, taught me that the soreness at acupressure points could be relieved painlessly with a very light touch plus a shift of focus.

I studied yoga and learned many breathing techniques, but my most valuable experience in this area came from learning Hawaiian breathing techniques from my *hanai* uncle, William Kahili, especially the technique called "piko-piko."

I learned a lot of guided imagery techniques from many sources in the seventies and eighties, but the most profound understanding and proficient use of this modality came out of my shamanic work with my Uncle William.

All of this can be considered the embyonic stages of DMT.

The actual birth of Dynamind was really a surprise to me, since I thought I was finished with developing healing techniques. After all, my book, *Instant Healing*, which I thought of at the time as the culmination of my healing knowledge and practice, was about to appear on the market and I

5

was ready to turn my mind to other things. The Universe, however, had different ideas.

Earlier in that same year I had given a workshop called "Huna Therapy," in which I presented several of the techniques from the *Instant Healing* book. Afterwards, one of the students of that workshop emailed me to express her pleasure with the course, and to suggest that I check out a website offering a completely different kind of healing technique. It turned out to be a site dedicated to Gary Craig's Emotional Freedom Technique (EFT). I was intrigued enough to order a set of his video tapes, and after watching them I was impressed enough to start a research program of my own.

Craig, whose system is based on the work of Dr. Roger Callahan, has developed a great technique and his whole approach is very much in keeping with the spirit of this book. As I experimented with his process, however, a lot of different ideas began running through my mind. First of all, I remembered that I had come across Callahan's work very briefly in the 1980s and that I had turned away from it because at the time I thought it was too complicated and illogical. Second, while EFT most definitely worked, I found that the effects were virtually identical to those of several Hawaiian-based techniques that I used on a regular basis. The difference was that in many cases EFT worked faster.

I had previously developed and used a number of fast healing techniques, such as PRDW, a verbal technique involving subconscious dialogue; Piko-Piko, involving deeper breathing with a shift of attention from point to point; a type of progressive desensitization using memory and tension release; symbolizing the problem and changing the symbol; and Kahi, a method combining touch and piko-piko. All of these are very successful and very fast, but EFT seemed to be even faster, plus more flexible and capable of working with a wider variety of problems. It also required less "work" on the part of the client in terms of recall, inner dialogue, behavioral change, etc.

Why should that be, I wondered? Craig and I used different techniques to get the same result even though we used different theories about the healing process. Yet his way often worked faster than mine. So instead of abandoning my ideas and techniques I just fiddled with them. What would happen if I modified my theories thus and so? What would happen if I modified my techniques, or if I combined them in a different way? How simple could the process be and still get results? My research notes are full of major and minor variations on the process while working with live clients in order to fulfill these specific criteria:

1. The technique had to be effective.

2. The technique had to be simple to learn and easy to remember.

3. The technique had to be based on a logical, demonstrable theory.

4. The technique had to incorporate familiar concepts (i.e., it had to combine existing techniques based on well-known processes).

5. The technique had to be flexible enough to combine with other treatments and processes.

6. The technique had to be as fast or faster than EFT in obtaining results (thank you, Gary, for your inspiration).

The final result was a process that combined several effective techniques from Hawaiian tradition into a new "recipe" based on very different concepts from those used in EFT and similar "energy" therapies.

By June, 2000, the Dynamind Technique was presented in a public workshop for the first time in Nuuk, Greenland. Following are the five live demonstrations that we did then. Each person mentioned was a volunteer from the audience. Note that a "round" consists of four steps in a process that takes less than thirty seconds to do.

Demo 1 - Doctor: several rounds relieved shoulder tension so much that she could not remember them ever having been so relaxed before.

Demo 2 - Nurse: several rounds reduced pain from cancer surgery, and later rounds relieved fear of the cancer coming back.

Demo 3 - Student: two rounds relieved knee tension.

Demo 4 - Architect: two rounds relieved anxiety.

Demo 5 - Teacher: several rounds relieved a feeling of heaviness in her legs.

Since that first workshop the Dynamind Technique has been taught to many thousands of people around the world, through videos, manuals, online instructions, more workshops, and an international team of Certified Dynamind Practitioners and Teachers. Our recorded case studies show that Dynamind has been effectively applied to the following sets of problems. The list is not complete because new applications are constantly being discovered:

Relief of Physical Pain and Aches
Back (upper, middle, lower)
Shoulders
Joints
Muscles (including myalgia)
Headaches and migraines
Neck pain and stiffness
Eye soreness
Teeth, gums and jaws
Bones
Skin
Heart

Tendons
Uterine, vaginal and cervical areas
Generalized pain
Relief of Other Physical Conditions
Numbness and tingling
Arthritis (pain, swelling, stiffness)
Cancer (relief of pain, nausea from treatment, related emotional issues)
Stiffness (joint and muscle)
Skin conditions (Dermatitis, Eczema, Hives, Swelling, Itching)
Allergy symptoms
Nausea (including seasickness)
Weight management (controlling urges)
Tinnitus
Ear pressure
Diabetic shakiness
Cold, sinus and flu symptoms
Shortness of breath
Fatigue and exhaustion
Weakness
Dizziness and Vertigo
Excess energy and nervousness
Excessive heat or burning sensations
Menopause symptoms (including hot flashes)
Insomnia
Vision Improvement (Nearsightedness, Farsightedness, Distortion)
General physical stress and tension

Emotional Pain and Feelings
Anxiety (specific and generalized)
Anger and resentment
Guilt and grief

Unhappiness
Depression
Loss
Abandonment
Betrayal
Sadness
Abuse
General emotional stress and tension

Mental Pain and Issues
Doubt
Confusion
Indecision
Conflict
Worry
Self Worth and Self Esteem
Criticism and negative thoughts
Nightmares
Autism
General mental stress and tension

Habits
Nail-biting
Smoking
Bed-wetting
Alcohol intake (urge control)
Over-eating (urge control and emotional aspects)

In the following pages you will learn the theory upon which the Dynamind Technique is based, a detailed analysis of every part of the technique itself, and an abundance of ways and means to apply the technique for solving inner and outer problems of health, wealth, happiness and success. Most of the information will be easily adapted to the everyday problems of most people in the world.

In addition to the application of Dynamind to familiar problems, some people are experimenting with more unusual applications that do not fit into our usual picture of the nature of reality. In spite of many questions raised by these experimental uses, I have included a chapter on them for you to speculate about.

For those of you who just can't wait, here is the text of the most basic form (only slightly expanded for those who are not familiar with it) from a card I hand out to clients:

The Basic Form of The Dynamind Technique

Say: "I have a problem and it can change. I want the problem to go away."

Tap seven times on your chest, the outside web of each hand, and the base of your neck.

Breath from the top of your head to your toes.

It is hard to get much more simple than that, but the best part is that it works whether you understand how it works or not. If you do want to understand how it works, read on.

Chapter One
A DIFFERENT THEORY
OF HEALING

There are only a few significant things that human beings everywhere have in common. Other than similar internal and external organs, a body design roughly based on the Golden Mean ratio of 1.618, and varied levels of memory and imagination, they also share in common certain specific patterns of reaction to the experience of life. These reaction patterns are consistent among all people, regardless of race, color, culture, or creed, although not everyone has the same reaction all the time to the same type of experience.

Of these reactions, the most important in terms of its effect on our lives, and perhaps the least understood, is called "stress." Since one of the most important effects of Dynamind is to relieve stress, let's study this reaction in a great deal more detail.

Stress And Dynamic Systems

Think of an orchestra playing a symphony on a summer night in an outdoor pavilion to an audience of a thousand people. The members of the orchestra are concentrating on their conductor, their instruments, their music sheets, and their neighboring musicians. At the same time, they are aware of and are being influenced by the audience, the night breezes, possibly insects, and the surrounding sounds of nature or city life, depending on their location. Suddenly, a gust of wind blows several music sheets off their stands in the middle of a performance. There is a scramble among the musicians affected to retrieve their music, while the rest of the orchestra falters a bit, regroups, and compensates as smoothly as it can until all the musicians and their music sheets are back in place and the playing of the piece continues as before.

Anything which is composed of different parts that are organized to carry out a specific purpose may be called a system. We may speak, therefore, of a railway system, a tunnel system, a distribution system, a sound system, and so on. However, these kinds of systems are static systems. That is, they are established by external forces (such as human beings) and when they experience disruption they have to be repaired by external forces (such as human beings). A dynamic system, by contrast, is self-organizing and self-repairing, even when influenced by external forces (human or otherwise), at least up to a point. An orchestra is a grouping of individual human beings for a specific purpose, and it has the capacity to organize itself and to repair itself in response to potential disruptions from the environment.

The quality of a dynamic system (like an orchestra) to respond to disruptions in its state (the breeze blowing away the sheet music) by restoring its flexible integrity through a coordinated response of its parts (some musicians retrieving the sheets and the other adjusting to their absence) in order to return to a previous dynamic state (being an orchestra) is called "homeostasis," meaning "similar state of balance."

Individual human beings are dynamic systems composed of multiple sub-systems (the nervous system, the respiratory system, the circulation system, the lymph system, etc.) and they also have the quality of homeostasis. In human beings, it refers to the way the body tries to resist changes to its current dynamic state, and immediately starts processes, such as healing, whenever disruption or change does occur, to return to a previous dynamic state.

Things that have the potential to cause disruption or change are called "stressors," and the reaction of resistance to stressors is called "stress." This statement is so important that I am going to repeat it in a different way. The stress we experience as human beings does not come from the disruptions, changes or influences that happen to us, or even from the ones that we ourselves happen to generate. Those things *might* produce stress effects, but they do not *necessarily* produce stress effects.

Excessive positive ions are a source of headaches and irritability for some people, but not for others. Criticism is a source of great stress for some people, but not for all people. Most people will probably experience painful burns from direct skin contact with fire, but some people can walk on fire with no effect whatsoever. Everyone is affected in some way by stressors, but some people are able to adapt or recover more quickly than others. Physical, emotional, or mental pain or discomfort only come from resisting forces that threaten to disrupt or change the personal system.

But why should a system resist change? What is it about change that stimulates the impulse to resist?

The most obvious answer is that without resistance to change, a system of any kind would become chaotic, and would therefore cease to exist as a system. In order for a dynamic system to continue as a system, it must have within itself the means to regain its integrity in the face of any but the most catastrophic levels of change. This is no more, and no less, than the principle of momentum in physics applied to dynamic systems. To remind you of what Sir Isaac Newton named as his first principle of motion:

"An object at rest tends to stay at rest and an object in

motion tends to stay in motion with the same speed and in the same direction unless acted upon by an unbalanced force."

Some people think that the last part of the above sentence says "...unless acted upon by an outside force," but Newton shows that an outside balanced force would have no effect on an object at rest or moving. And, interestingly, Newton does not even say that the unbalanced force needs to come from outside the object, a very important concept that I will bring up again.

In the case of dynamic, open systems, like the human body, a very similar principle applies. We could put it this way:

"A dynamic, open system tends to maintain its integrity as a system unless acted upon by an unbalanced force, in which case it seeks to restore its integrity if it can, and ceases to be a system if it cannot."

Stressing, i.e., resisting a stressor, is one of the ways in which any object or system tries to maintain its integrity. Dynamic, open systems, like the body, have the additional capability of restoration, which for practical purposes can also be called "healing," as a means of bringing integrity back, up to a point. In the orchestra example above, integrity was restored after the breeze blew off the sheet music. If one or more members of the orchestra became sick and had to go home, the orchestra would try to function as such as long as it could, until so many members were lost that it could not be an orchestra any more. The same thing happens to people. They will keep adapting to "unbalanced forces" for as long as they can still function as human beings. Or they will resist such forces for as long as they can. The way that people respond to stressors, or "unbalanced forces," is important to know in order to understand how healing relates to stress.

As human beings we have two primary dynamic sub-systems that make up our whole human being system, and four responses to unbalanced forces which threaten the integrity of these systems.

Two Sub-Systems

First, there is the physical system, which means our body. As a dynamic system it is constantly changing itself and responding to changes in its inner and outer environment, and all of this takes place within a broad pattern of functional behavior that we can call "being alive." Being alive, of course, is not necessarily the same as being healthy, because the physical dynamic system includes a very wide range of possible states or levels of functioning within which a recognizably living body can exist. "Being alive" can mean existing in a coma while machines help to maintain basic body functions, or it can mean existing in a state of bliss and seemingly miraculous powers of healing. And everything in between, of course.

Second, there is the mental system, which means our mind. There are those who claim that the mind is merely an effect of the body, but that has to be the silliest idea that any apparently intelligent human being has ever come up with. It's equivalent to saying that airplanes and computers and religions and philosophies and even healing techniques are all no more than by-products of bodily functions, and that is so absurd that I'm not going to discuss it any more.

Even though the mind is so intangible that we cannot explain it in terms of physics or biology, and even though it cannot be explained metaphysically in terms clear enough for everyone to understand, anyone who remembers, thinks, and imagines has experience with what we call the mind. Yet, in spite of its intangibility the mind behaves like a dynamic system. We can notice this most easily when we assume that beliefs form the underlying "structure" of the mind, just as cells form the underlying structure of the body. The belief system tends to resist change, while at the same time there is an urge to learn that promotes the adapting, modifying or changing of beliefs. Like the body, the mind tries to retain its integrity as it responds to unbalanced outside forces like new experiences and the ideas of other people.

Both body and mind respond to stressors in very similar ways.

Four Responses To Stressors

The four responses to stressors that I propose include the two well-known resistant forms called "fight" and "flight," as well as two lesser known adaptive forms called "peace" and "play." Each of these are natural responses that can be applied in positive ways, and each one of them also has negative potential. In the modern world, the use of the first two has been exaggerated far out of proportion to their potential benefits.

"Fight," as can be guessed, is a stress response of trying to push away a stressor, trying to forcibly change it, or trying to destroy it. Physical examples would include hitting someone who bothers you, making an active child sit still for your convenience, or tearing apart a book that you don't agree with. Mental examples would be arguing angrily against an idea you don't like, criticising someone to make them change their ways, or gossiping about someone in order to ruin their reputation. The two main problems with the fight response are that it tends to cause so much tension that your own dynamic system may become unstable, and it tends to increase the resistant behavior of any other dynamic systems you are fighting. In other words, when you use a fight response as a reaction to other people, oddly enough they tend to fight back.

17

"Flight" is a response of trying to run away from a stressor, trying to avoid it, or trying to suppress it. Physical examples of interest to us here would be running away from home because you feel unloved, becoming an alcoholic so you don't have to deal with emotional conflicts, or forcing yourself to stay in a relationship that you don't like. Mental examples would be using meditation or day-dreaming to escape from your problems, distracting yourself with television so you don't have to do things you don't want to do, or pretending to be indifferent when you are hurting inside. Like the fight response, flight generates tension that may make your system unstable. Unlike fight, the flight response tends to create a barrier between you and other people, making them even more likely to draw away from you.

Flight and fight responses are very often mixed in a single system. The urge to hit someone in anger may be suppressed by fear to the point where a person might develop bursitis in his or her shoulder. A fear of expressing anger may initiate epileptic seizures or ritualistic behavior. A human dynamic system that is angry at itself and that fears itself at the same time can produce devastating consequences for health and well-being.

The "Peace" response is one of tolerating the stressor to the point where it ceases to be a stressor, or of integrating it into the system for the same effect. Physical examples are the way we stop noticing a bad odor after awhile, easily setting an extra place at the table when a friend brings a stranger to dinner, or willingly eating a food you don't like because of its nutritional benefits. Mental examples are the adjustment we make to a friend moving out of town, deciding to let your children decorate their own rooms, or accepting a new son-in-law or daughter-in-law into the family. Because the Peace response is adaptive and not resistive, any tension provoked by a stressor tends to be quickly dispersed. However, it may be possible for tolerance for or adaptation to people or circumstances to go so far as to threaten the integrity of the system, in which case Fight or Flight may kick in for subconscious self-preservation, such as when another person's behavior becomes so destructive that a Peace response is no longer a viable option.

The "Play" response is one of temporarily or permanently using the stressor to benefit the system, in which case it also ceases to be a stressor to any great degree. Physical examples are using a physical handicap to inspire others with the same problem, turning physical exercise into an enjoyable habit, or making a game of hard work. Mental examples are learning how to heal your illness, writing a book about a personal crisis, or turning your anquish into art. The only potential negative effect of the Play response occurs when you cease to enjoy whatever you are doing. That is when Fight or Flight take over. In the business and professional world today this is referred to as "burn-out."

The first two responses result in a great deal of temporary or chronic tension, and the second two do not. Everyone uses all four to some degree, but most societies today emphasize the development of fight or flight skills much more than they do those of peace-making or play. According to my theoretical structure all four are natural responses, and each has their proper time and place to be used. However, since most of our personal and social problems come from an overuse of fight or flight, a lot of the information in this book will be directed toward healing the effects of that overuse.

Three Types Of Stressors

Stressors that affect the body or the mind are always energetic in nature. That is, it is only the energy evoked or provoked by the potential stressor that may cause a stress reaction. A hammer will not produce a stress reaction just by being a hammer. If it is wielded against a finger purposely or accidentally it probably will, or if it raises up an energetically traumatic memory it probably will, but if it just casually lies about in a calm state of hammerness it probably will not. Also, the personal perception of the strength of a stressor depends on the current stress state of the system. The more stress a system is currently experiencing, the more easily it may respond to any additional experience as a stressor. At one time in my life when I was in a state of extreme stress I had to keep my eyes closed, because even the sight of all the objects in a darkened room was too much for me to bear. In that case it was not the objects themselves, but the energy of their dim, reflected light that I could not stand.

There are three general types of stressors that we respond to: Physical, Emotional, and Mental. The most important thing to understand about stressors is that, regardless of their origin, they always stress both our physical and our mental dynamic systems according to how much we resist them.

Physical stressors are the things that directly affect us through our physical senses of sight, sound, touch, taste, and smell. Emotional stressors are the so-far unmeasurable energies of other people's emotions and the energetic effects of our own emotions. Mental stressors are the thoughts and ideas of others as well as the ones we produce ourselves.

In the next two sections I am going to discuss how the body and the mind typically react to stressors when engaged in a fight or flight response. Emotional reactions will be discussed in the chapters on Anger and Fear.

The Physical Stress Reaction

Remember that a stress reaction refers to the behavior of resisting a stressor.

A lot of different things happen in the body at the same time when a stress reaction occurs. Although I am going to discuss them one by one, keep in mind that these reactions are happening simultaneously. Also, please keep in mind that I am greatly simplifying the process, because this is not a textbook on physiology. And one more thing: almost everything we think we know about how the human body functions is based on theory, so don't be surprised if every health practitioner doesn't agree with my version of things.

Muscle Tension. Muscles are composed of elongated cells that respond to stimulation, usually neural, by contracting or stretching, and then relaxing to their original shape. Basically, their function is to provide motion, to maintain posture, and to produce heat. Since some kinds of muscles line the organs, the blood vessels, and the eyes, strong stimulation can cause acute or chronic contractions that inhibit organ function or restrict blood and lymph circulation in these areas, too.

During a stress reaction, muscle contractions may also distort facial expressions and posture, induce shallow and/or rapid breathing, increase heart rate and blood pressure, and distort vision, to name just a few effects.

Blood Vessel Dilation. Blood vessels, which include veins, arteries, and capillaries, are structured like tubes of tightly-woven netting. When the body stresses, these blood vessels dilate, or expand, perhaps to allow for an increase in the flow of blood to working cells. Under too much stress, however, they dilate to the extent that the fluid they carry begins to spill out into the surrounding cells. The first part of the blood to spill through the net is water, which is why any degree of stress reaction produces a certain amount of dehydration. The greater the stress, the more dehydrated you get, until the dehydration itself acts as a stressor, causing even stronger stress reactions. The next major fluid loss under stress is blood plasma, the clear part of the blood that contains, among other things, white blood cells and protein. When plasma spills out among the surrounding cells it may prevent oxygen from reaching the cells, causing varying levels of localized discomfort or pain.

The most dramatic loss of fluid involves blood vessel dilation to such a degree that the larger red blood cells themselves spill out of the net. This is what causes the more severe stress reaction of "blood draining from his face," or "turning white as a ghost." There are instances in which red blood cell loss during stress has been so great that blood transfusions were required.

Heart Rate Increase. The heart is a muscle, of course, but it is constantly stretching and contracting in order to pump blood through our circulatory system. Like other muscles, strong stressors can cause it to contract or stretch excessively, but the heart's most common stress reaction is to beat faster. The healthy aspect of this is to get more blood to areas of the body that need it as quickly as possible. The unhealthy aspect is that if those areas are under a great deal of tension themselves, the increased heart rate and blood pressure can have unpleasant side effects.

Thymus Contraction. The thymus is a small, flattish gland located in the upper center of the chest, and it plays a major role in the production of white blood cells, and therefore in the immune system as a whole. Although it is usual to say that the thymus gland itself is contracting during a stress reaction, it may be that the chest muscles around it are doing the real contracting. Nevertheless, the result is a diminishing of white blood cell production and, depending on the severity of the reaction, sensations ranging from mild tightness to acute pain.

Energy Consumption. Glucose is a sugar, and for most people it is the basic fuel that the body burns for maintenance, growth, repair, and activity. Glucose is also the primary fuel used by the brain. There is always a small amount of glucose in the bloodstream for the body's immediate use, but most of it is stored in the form of glycogen, mainly in the liver and to some degree in the muscles. People on low-carbohydrate/high protein-fat diets such as most Inuits, Mongolians, Berbers and Atkins followers use fatty acids for more of their energy, but they still need some glucose or they have other stress-related problems. As part of the stress response, additional glucose is released from the liver and muscles in preparation for intense activity. Since the hormone adrenaline is what causes the sugar to be released, this effect is often called an "adrenaline rush." Because having too much sugar in the bloodstream for too long can damage blood cells if the sugar fuel is not used up quickly enough, the pancreas, another gland, discharges insulin into the bloodstream to neutralize the glucose. In a prolonged stress situation, glucose and insulin levels can go back and forth, causing all kinds of health problems.

Pain Sensations. Stress responses often produce sensations of pain in various parts of the body, and the pain itself may also become a stressor, causing more stress reactions. There is no generally accepted theory about the cause of pain, but it is commonly thought that all pain sensations come from over-stimulated or damaged nerves. However, new research suggests otherwise. A condition called Tension Myositis Syndrome, involving connections between emotions, the limbic system, the brain, and the autonomic nervous system has been proposed by Dr. John Sarno of New York University's Rusk Institute as the source of much of the body's pain experiences. The work of Dr. Majid Ali, Professor of Medicine at the Capital University of Integrative Medicine in New York proposes oxygen deprivation at the cellular level as the source of pain and many other symptoms of stress. My own complementary theory, based entirely on empirical studies, is that physical tension is the direct cause of pain, whether because it impinges on nerves or inhibits the supply of oxygen to the cells. Theories on what causes pain will be dealt with more completely in Chapter Three.

Endorphin Release. Stress responses, including pain, release natural biochemicals called endorphins which help to reduce the perception of pain, enhance the immune response, and activate feelings of well-being. Of course, if the stress response is strong enough we might not notice the endorphin effect, but it is very likely that stress and pain symptoms would feel a lot worse without it. In addition to stress and pain, endorphins are known to be secreted as a result of eating chocolate and chili peppers, engaging in strenuous atheletic activities, or experiencing acupuncture, massage, sex or meditation. Also, different people may produce different levels of endorphin release during similar experiences.

These are some of the major things that occur in your body in any kind of stress reaction, no matter what the cause. Now we'll look at the mental system.

The Mental Stress Reaction

Like the body, the mind is also a dynamic system. It, too, tries to maintain a state of homeostasis by resisting or adapting to changes in its current dynamic state by unbalanced forces from within and without. Although the mind and body may be thought of as distinct systems, each with their own responses to stressors, they are not separate, any more than the circulatory system is separate from the nervous system, or the orchestra is separate from its listening audience. In fact, the body can play the role of healing agent or stressor for the mind, and the mind can be healer or stressor for the body.

Whenever there is a physical symptom of stress there is an equivalent, but not necessarily equal, mental symptom, and vice versa. With that said, let's look at some of the things that happen when the mind resists a stressor. Remember, these are common to all people everywhere to varying degrees. The difference between the mind and the body systems is that not all of these symptoms will occur with everyone all the time.

Forgetfulness. In a stress state the mind begins to forget things. In my view, memories are energy patterns, somewhat like data in computers, and the body stores these memories in the cells that that were stimulated when a particular event took place. If tension in the body is enough to inhibit the movement of these cells, then the memories they store are inaccessible, at least temporarily. I am writing this book on a deadline, which, like it or not, causes me some degree of stress. So, about an hour ago I was trying to think of a particular word I wanted to use in a sentence and it would not come to me, even though I knew I knew it. A few moments ago, while thinking of something else, my wife asked me if I had remembered the word, and in that moment it came back to me, because in that moment the part of my body in which that word was stored was relaxed.

The more stress a person is experiencing in the body, the more difficult it is to access memory, and extreme stress in the body may produce extreme memory deprivation. The mind is also capable of forgetting what it doesn't want to remember, and when the mind is thinking angry or fearful thoughts the resulting tension in the body may also inhibit memory recall.

One effect of this phenomenon that few people consider is that all of our knowledge, habits and skills are based on memory. This means that when your body is experiencing a high enough level of tension you may not be able to access the memories of coping or healing skills that you have learned. It doesn't matter how much you know about healing, or how well you have learned to apply self-healing skills if your tension is such that you can't remember them. When this happens it is very useful to swallow pride and get some outside help.

Confusion. This is related to forgetfulness because it is related to memory access, but the experience is different. In a state of confusion, either what you are experiencing doesn't make sense, or you find yourself unable make logical connections or clear decisions. The main factor is that the memories which bind things seem to be missing. In a normal state, if you saw a chair in a hallway you would either remember having put it there or you would make a reasonable guess that someone else had put it there for some reason. In a confused state you might not be able to comprehend any possible reason for that chair to be there or you would not be able to make a decision as to what to do about it, and in a highly confused state you might not be able to understand what kind of object it was or what it could possibly be used for. The associative links would not be available because tension would be blocking the memories.

Boredom. When you are bored with work, play, your environment or your life, that is a clear sign of mental stress, which means you are resisting something that you feel is either threatening your dynamic mental system, or failing to nourish it.

Fairly recently, boredom has been given a more medically significant name: Attention Deficit Disorder, and that opens it up to being treatable by drugs, of course. While it's true that some people may actually need medical help with this problem, it's also true that ADD is often used as an excuse to justify fundamentally boring conditions at work, school or elsewhere. When I was in the third grade I got into serious trouble because the teacher would always find me drawing cartoons in my notebook rather than reading the lesson. The fact was that I had been reading since I was three years old, and I had read the lesson five times before the other students had finished going through it once. The teacher wouldn't believe that, however, and so I was punished, which didn't exactly improve my love of schoolwork.

Nevertheless, boredom is a stress reaction, and if not relieved it can grow into much more disfunctional levels of apathy and withdrawal.

Divergency. As a mental condition, this is the active opposite of concentration. "Attention Deficit Hyperactive Disorder" is the popular modern term, but that's such a clumsy phrase. A state of divergency is when a person is unable to maintain attention for very long on one topic or one task, and it is a stress response of the Flight type. Curiously, at higher stress levels, attempting to forcibly modify this pattern often results in a Fight response, as if divergency had become a coping system of its own within the larger mental system and its integrity felt threatened. This is one explanation for the agressiveness some hyperactive children show when attempts are made to calm them down.

Hypercriticism. Most people simply call this "negative thinking." Criticism itself is just a very inefficient technique for trying to make things better. Parents critcize children and teachers criticize students based on a tragically mistaken and totally unproven theory that this will somehow turn them into happier children or better students. Hypercriticism is a Fight type of stress response that takes criticism to exaggerated levels by refusing to see good in anything or anyone, or by actively seeking out and making known the bad.

Distraction. The human mind is incredibly

creative, even in the ways it devises to deal with stress. Distraction is a Flight type of stress response that tries to hide a great fear of something by making something else very important and very difficult to deal with. In that way the person can avoid thinking about what they really fear, and often what they fear is their own anger. The most common forms that this response takes are Obsessions, Compulsions, Depressions, and Phobias. Sometimes, however, the original fear fades away and the distraction behavior remains as an inconvenient habit.

Obsessions are topics, other persons, or activities that people become so involved in that they neglect other important areas of life, or they get themselves into social or legal difficulties. Compulsions are specific behaviors, like hand-washing or not stepping on cracks, that keep a person too occupied to think about their primary fear. Depression is a type of reaction of helpless anger toward a fearful situation of some kind. Phobias are specific fears that focus on avoiding someone or something that is usually not inherently threatening, but which helps them avoid another fear. One may have a phobia in regard to something potentially dangerous, of course, but such phobias are always exaggerated expressions of what might be a normal fear response.

Displacement. When someone is highly stressed and is unable to vent his or her anger against the real object of this feeling, then the distorted mental Fight response of Displacement may occur. In this case the anger, ranging from mild irritation to all-consuming rage, may be displaced toward an alternate object which is either safer or more convenient to act against. A typical example often used is that of a man who is angry with his boss and comes home to kick the dog (or slap his wife or beat the kids). Rages in particular are set off by a combination of high physical stress levels and rules for other people's behavior, the breaking of which releases great anger against something easier to deal with than whatever the person feels helpless about.

Stress Layers

I first mentioned this idea briefly in my book, *Urban Shaman*, where I used the alternate term "tension layers." It comes from a "working" theory that physical tension accumulates in layers. A "working" theory is one that is used because it is useful, and not because it necessarily conforms to accepted facts. As far as I know, stress layers do not make any sense physiologically, any more than Chinese acupuncture meridians do, yet in both cases the assumption of their existence is useful to the healing process.

In thousands of cases of helping people to heal themselves around the world I have observed that healing one symptom by whatever means either reduces the intensity of that symptom, eliminates it entirely, or results in its replacement by another symptom in the same location or elsewhere.

Many people who work with pain relief, for example, have noted a phenomenon which they usually describe as "chasing the pain." What this means is that when they relieve pain in one place, pain mysteriously appears in another place. The assumption used in this case is that the pain is a discrete entity with a will of its own that must be hunted down in order to be eliminated. And if it is finally eliminated, and pain appears again on another day, it is said that "the pain came back," as if it were merely on holiday, or waiting around the corner to jump back in at the first opportunity.

I find that this concept by itself generates more stress than it relieves, because it tends to make those who suffer from pain, especially recurring pain, feel unnecessarily fearful and helpless.

Physiologically, pain is an effect, not a thing, just as an ocean wave is an effect of wind, and not a thing that you can pick up and carry home. Theoretically, pain is an effect of stress and, just like the fact that a wave disappears when the wind calms down, so does pain disappear when stress is relieved.

In the stress layer theory, tension occurs in the body from the inside out, with the most recent layers on or near the surface of the skin. The more tension there is in a particular layer, the more that tension tends to concentrate in a particular area, thus producing a localized symptom. Therefore, relieving the tension of a top layer relieves any associated symptom completely and permanently. The next layer down may have its tension concentrated in the same place in the same form, in the same place with a different form, in a different place with the same form, or in a different place with a different form. The simple figure below will illustrate what I mean.

_____	*headache	
_____	*headache	
	*shoulder pain	
	*nausea	
		*knee trembles

As the headaches are relieved a shoulder pain appears; when that is gone there is nausea in the stomach area; when that is gone the knees begin to tremble. The symptoms act as if they were on layers (or at least that is the way I choose to interpret the phenomena). The good thing is that when a person does the Dynamind Technique with this theory in mind, he or she can calmly relieve symptoms as they appear until the whole body feels good. And the best part is that the symptoms are being lessened or disappearing as a result of relieving tension in the body, which affects the whole body, and not just the area of the symptom.

The final part of the layers theory is that old symptoms never reappear. What happens is that new stress generates new symptoms on new layers of tension. One of the side benefits of this theory is that a person can learn how to change physical, emotional or mental behavior in order in order to prevent old forms of symptoms from being generated again for the same reasons.

However, when a particular part of the body has been severely traumatized, it seems to be easier for the body to generate new symptoms in the same area, probably because it learned how to do that very well at the time of the trauma. We can say that such areas are more sensitive to stress. When I was three or four years old I fell out of a moving car on a highway at night. I can still remember sitting there looking at the cars and trucks whizzing by me. What I do not remember consciously was the fact that my left collarbone was broken. Since then, throughout my life, whenever I get stressed for any reason, my left shoulder tightens up. And when that happens, I simply relieve the tension.

Stress Channels

What I call a "Stress Channel" is whatever there is in your life that you have a strong tendency to get stressed about. Typical Stress Channel categories are people, places, things, activities and ideas.

People. A woman named Alice Steadman once wrote a book with the great title, *Who's The Matter With Me*, to emphasize the connection between our reactions to people and the state of our health. Usually, the people you stress most about include your family, your friends, your co-workers, and whatever bureaucrats you have to deal with, but there are those who also stress about anyone who is different from them. Notice how carefully I phrased that. The majority of people automatically assume that other people cause them stress. My theory says that you are the one who is causing the stress, by your reaction to them. It might be a useful exercise to think about the most important people in your life and check on how and where your body reacts when you think about them.

Places. Some people stress about their home, their neighborhood, their city, their workplace, overhead power lines, nearby factories, or any other place that stirs up associations and reactions.

Things. Some people stress about specific things that they don't like, such as furniture, paintings, junk or clutter, whether it belongs to them or not. Doing something to remove or clean up the objects you don't like is one way to relieve the stress; another is changing your reaction to it.

Activities. Work, no matter how much or how little you get paid for it, is one of the major stress channels for most people. Even sports can be stress-provoking, especially competitive sports, and relieving these kinds of stress reactions can have a large impact on your health.

Ideas. It is amazing how stressed people can get in relation to something as non-physical as an idea, particularly when it has to do with religion, politics, philosophy, education, science, or health. It is one thing to discuss ideas, another to debate them, and quite another to turn purple in the face and nearly have a stroke when you enounter ones you don't like. It's also a good idea to check your body's reactions to ideas of various kinds.

The most important thing to remember is that mental stress responses produce physical stress responses in the body, and mental stress responses in the mind. Furthermore, physical stress responses tend to stress the mind, and mental stress responses tend to stress the body. If you can find a way to change the response patterns of your mind and your body at the same time, then you can produce some remarkable healings. In the next chapter we'll analyze the Dynamind Technique to see how it can help you do that.

Considerations

Even when Dynamind is effective, some people will object to it because of other theories they may have about the healing process. Everyone has a right to their own theory, of course, but I'd like to comment on some of the most frequent objections.

The Theory of Necessary Difficulty. Most often this is stated as "It can't be that easy!" This theory has a very large number of followers who are convinced that healing requires a lot of time and effort, and a great percentage of those believe that a certain amount of suffering is needed, too. The speed and simplicity of the Dynamind Technique is shocking to these people. Some will refuse to try it; some will try it while aborting the process with sustained skepticism; and some will try it, get great results, and then become so uncomfortable or afraid that they have somehow done something wrong by healing so quickly and easily that they will spend considerable time re-stressing themselves in order to bring the symptoms back.

Part of the problem is that they do not have a familiar context into which they can put the experience, since most traditional and conventional techniques do take more time, effort, and personal sacrifice in the form of additional pain or a lot more money. Faith healing is a familiar context for some of these people, but Dynamind does not require faith and therefore remains out of context. As long as you are not adamantly skeptical, Dynamind will still work for most people most of the time even when they don't expect any results at all.

The Difficulty Theory is also followed by people who do not want healing to be easy. One portion of this group believes, consciously or subconsciously, that suffering is a kind of spiritual punishment or trial and that if healing takes great struggle and sacrifice they will be a better person for it. Another portion, sadly enough, consists of health practitioners who see rapid healing in terms of lost income. Actually, I can understand that, because if everyone in a particular country were to use Dynamind every day − or any of the other rapid healing techniques available − as a first treatment for every health issue they have to deal with, there would probably be a tremendous drop in visits to hospitals and clinics, as well as a substantial decrease in the sales of medicines.

Rather than trying to change the minds of these people, we need to be tolerant of their right to believe what they want, and of our right to pursue what we believe is best for us.

The Theory of Distraction. One of the objections I have heard about Dynamind is that is is merely a distraction technique. In other words, the positive effect is supposed to be due to the fact that the process distracts the client or subject from the problem and a healing takes place by itself.

This idea has a small amount of substance, so for that reason I am going to quote myself from a response I gave to one of our Practitioners about this very issue: "In healing, distraction gives the mind and body a rest period from the problem. Sometimes mental or physical behavior is changed spontaneously during this rest period, as when a child falls and cries and is distracted by a piece of candy. Sometimes the problem behavior returns immediately after the distraction because no internal change was made, as when a sick person laughs at a joke, but doesn't get well.

"In Dynamind, the attention is first directed immediately to the problem, often in great detail. There is certainly no distraction in this. Then a new decision about the problem is made, and there is no distraction in this, either. Next, a form of tension release is used which does have an element of distraction in it, but then the attention is brought right back to the problem in a very analytical way. In most cases, as you have found, this combination of a focus on the problem, a potentially-distracting process of tension release, and a refocus on the problem generally produces a reduction or elimination of the symptoms. It is not the distraction itself that produces the change. If nothing else is done, when a distracted person goes back to the problem it will be the same.

"The change in Dynamind takes place during the tension release, which may be distracting for some people. Obviously, if the person continues an inner focus on maintaining the problem there will be no change. What makes any healing technique work, including Dynamind, is a change in mental and/or physical behavior. Dynamind uses decision-making, an element of distraction in the tension release, and an analysis of the results to accomplish this."

The Theory of Hidden Meaning. A significant number of people believe that all symptoms of physical and mental suffering are only surface manifestations of deeply-hidden beliefs, traumatic memories, or karmic impulses that require an expert to uncover, the way an archeologist digs into the earth to uncover a lost city. If you do not discover the "source" of the symptoms, say the proponents of this theory, then any symptom relief is both illusory and transitory. Unless you find the meaning of the problem or learn the "lesson" that the problem has to teach you, any true healing cannot happen.

My alternative view is that the symptoms are the problem, and the only thing that is hidden is an individual's awareness of the relationship between the symptoms and specific physical and/or mental behavior. Change the behavior and you solve the problem. This viewpoint is neither new nor mine alone. In the words of George Ivanovitch Gurdjieff, a philosopher and spiritual teacher of the early twentieth century, "The only purpose of suffering is to learn how not to suffer." It is my personal opinion that the search for hidden meanings in our suffering is a kind of game people play to delay the healing process. On the other hand, I am all for allowing people to play whatever game they choose, as long as I am not required to join in.

The Theory of Suggestibility. This theory is based on an assumption that people in general are helpless puppets, subject to the whim and will of anyone who suggests anything. According to this theory, all I would have to do to get a healing result with Dynamind would be to suggest to someone that it would work and they would immediately fall all over themselves to get well.

I wish. If suggestion worked that way we would all have health, wealth, happiness, success and peace already. After all, if anyone were to suggest something bad, someone else could just suggest something good. If suggestion worked that way I would suggest that everyone reading this book send me half their income for the rest of my life so I could buy a trip to the moon and live in luxury for the rest of my life. Are you getting out your checkbook, yet?

Having been a professional hypnotherapist for many years, I can tell you that people only accept suggestions that correspond to something they already want or believe is possible. In practice, that means that the suggestion has to be both desirable and logical. And even then they might not accept it because it conflicts with a different desire or another kind of logic. What helps to make Dynamind so effective is that it relies on physically-reinforced self-suggestion. Dynamind is something that you do for yourself, even when someone else is guiding you through the process. In those special cases where Dynamind is done by one person to help or influence another person, it only works when the "suggestion" is both received and accepted by the intended recipient. To paraphrase a saying used in astrology, "Suggestions only impel, they do not compel."

The Seven Principles of Healing

The Dynamind Technique was founded on Huna philosophy, a way of thinking that comes from Hawaii. Here are seven ideas about healing derived from that philosophy.

1. Health is our natural state, and Healing is our natural inclination. It takes more effort to be ill than to be healthy.

2. Health is influenced by physical, emotional, mental and spiritual experiences. You can change the mind to change the body, and change the body to change the mind.

3. Health is influenced by positive and negative focus. Positive purposes, goals, plans, intentions and benefits increase healing.

4. Health and illness are created daily, even hourly. They do not come from the past - only from present thinking about the past, present or future.

5. Healing is increased by love, received or given. Love includes tolerance, forgiveness, appreciation, friendship, pleasure, passion, joy and bliss.

6. Healing is increased by power, received or given. Power includes skill, authority, energy, trust, and confidence.

7. Healing is increased by any combination of words, images, feelings and action which is in harmony with the beliefs and expectations of the healee.

Chapter Two
THE ANATOMY OF
A TECHNIQUE

The fundamental structure of the Dynamind Technique consists of a sequence of Steps that form a Round. The Steps are:

1. The Gesture.
2. The Statement, to which a Symbol may or may not be added.
3. The Touch.
4. The Breath.

This chapter will elaborate on the concepts behind the technique itself, as well as each of the above steps.

The Role Of Authority

All physical, emotional, mental, and circumstantial problems are related to excessive tension in the body, caused by resistance to experience. Healing and change occur when the tension is reduced or eliminated, because as the tension is released the body and the mind automatically begin to re-establish homeostasis. Tension which produces undesirable symptoms is generally called "stress," so the process of healing and inducing positive change by reducing tension may also be called "stress relief" or "stress reduction."

The beneficial effect of any healing modality is directly related to the degree of stress relief it produces. It doesn't matter whether the modality is traditional, conventional, alternative or radical, nor does it matter whether the intervention is physical, emotional, mental, energetic, environmental, spiritual or unknown. The only thing that matters in terms of healing is how well the modality reduces stress. In this respect, surgery, medicine, and psychotherapy may be just as valid as acupuncture, therapeutic touch, past life regression and prayer. There are thousands of healing modalities in use around the world. Some are more complicated than others, some produce healing effects faster than others. Some require more preparation and practice than others.

In saying that healing modalities of whatever kind are effective to the degree that they relieve stress, it must be kept in mind that the stress itself is related to physical resistance on the part of the person experiencing the stress, whom I call the healee. Therefore, the reduction of stress must by directly related to the reduction of resistance. The latter is achieved by appealing to the healee's respect for authority.

"Authority" in this context refers to some aspect of the healing modality that activates the healee's expectation of a positive outcome for the intervention. The potential aspects in which individuals may invest authority include an extremely wide range of variation, which may explain why so many different kinds of interventions in different cultures can have equivalent effects, even when based on extremely varied theories of how they function.

Cultural bias promotes the fiction that a successful method of healing based on one culture's assumptions will necessarily be just as successful in other cultures. It may be successful to some degree in a different culture, but it will always have better results in the culture that produced it, as long as that culture continues to give authority to the method. Acupuncture, for instance, works better in China than it does elsewhere. Synthetic pharmaceuticals work better in the countries that developed them. The interventions of Filipino psychic healers work better in the Phillipines. Shamanic rituals work better among shamanically-oriented peoples. On the other hand, those types of treatment that involve elements common to all people, such as surgery, are more likely to be successful in fairly equal measure regardless of cultural differences.

The Dynamind Technique is based on the concept that it is possible to focus on a standard set of authoritative aspects which are generally recognized by most individuals of whatever race or culture, and to combine these aspects into a technique that will provide healing benefits to most of the people most of the time. Four such authoritative aspects shared by everyone are physical sensation, words, energetic sensation, and symbols. These are what constitute the structure of the Dynamind Technique.

On The Use Of Physical Sensation

This section will address the "Gesture" step of the Technique.

Physical postures and hand gestures are used around the world for communication, for self-expression, for ritual, and for entering different physical, emotional and mental states. The last two uses are the ones that interest us here.

Quite aside from any cultural uses of ritual is the fact that ritual behavior always serves to focus attention on the ritual itself, while at the same time diverting attention away from whatever is not pertinent to the ritual. When you are engaged in the ritual of dancing with a partner, your attention is naturally centered more on the music, the movements, and the interaction between you and your partner, and less on the surrounding environment. The effect is similar for any kind of ritual.

When teaching ritual as a process, I put great emphasis on having the students learn the first rule of good ritual, which is that you must have a clear beginning that captures the attention of those who will be involved in the ritual. It is this attention to the process that helps ensure whatever success the ritual is capable of providing. Neglect of this rule diminishes the effectiveness of any ritual, whether spiritual or secular. With a little practice, one can enter a state of meditation at will, without any preparation at all, yet even masters of meditation will use some preparatory step whenever they can, such as sitting in a particular way, holding their hands in a particular way, or breathing in a particular way. It is possible to begin a secular ritual like a meeting by just starting to talk, but professional meeting leaders will always use an attention-getting device like a gavel, a bell or even a loud announcement before getting on with the business of the meeting, because it helps to make a better meeting. Korean shamans move in and out of different altered states so fast it can make your head spin, but each change of state is preceded by a very quick costume change that helps the change of focus.

Capturing the attention for ritual requires some kind of action or experience that makes a sensory impression on the participants. Since the Dynamind Technique can be looked at as a type of ritual, I wanted to include such a beginning in the process. As with other rituals, this preparatory step is not vital. It is, however, extremely useful for increasing the effectiveness of the technique.

In my search for simplicity and effectiveness, I tried and discarded many types of beginnings, from special sounds and postures to visual and mental imagery. Some I discarded because they took too long or were unnecessarily complicated; some because they required an external tool or object; some because they were too contrived and added nothing to the Technique; some because they were too culturally limited; and some because, even though they were helpful, the Technique worked perfectly well without them.

Finally, I settled on a hand position that is not widely used; has very little, if any, cultural or religious significance; is different enough to attract attention, yet not so strange that it is likely to provoke resistance; and has the added benefit of helping to induce a pleasant state of calm relaxation when used by itself.

This nameless Gesture consists of bringing the fingertips of both hands together to form a hollow globe. It doesn't really matter where in front of the body this gesture is held, though for the sake of comfort it can be in the lap while sitting and close to the navel while standing. The Gesture is used for the purpose of centering at the beginning of the Technique, during the Statement, and during the Breath. Letting go of the Gesture signifies the end of a Round.

Sometimes, however, conditions are such that it may be very inconvenient to use the above hand position, as when driving a car, carrying something, or surrounded by people who would probably not understand what you were doing. On these occasions I still recommend some kind of special gesture to signify the start of the process, even though it might not be absolutely necessary. Two workable alternatives are to press the thumb and forefinger of one hand together for a moment, or to press any finger against a tangible surface momentarily. It still helps to prepare your subconscious for doing something special.

On The Use Of Words

Words have great authority among all human beings

who use them, or hear them, or see them. The words spoken or written by a person who has authority in the minds of those who read or listen to them have greater effect than those of persons of lesser authority.

In discussing his learning system called "Suggestology," Gregor Lozanov told about an experiment he did in which students were given two poems to memorize: one by a very famous Russian poet, and one by a poet who was virtually unknown. The students easily memorized the poem by the famous poet, but had great difficulty with the poem by the unknown one. The tricky part was that Lozanov had switched the poems. The students had no trouble with the poem that they thought was by the famous poet, and lots of trouble with the poem that they thought was by the unknown. By this and other similar experiments Lozanov made it clear that memorization ability is largely dependent on the authority given to the source of the material to be memorized.

In the United States, tremendous authority is given to the words of well-known celebrities, even out-of-work and very elderly celebrities. Because of this they are often hired to endorse all kinds of products on television, based on the assumption that if they say it's good, it must be good.

Although written words by recognized authority figures may have a significant impact, the spoken word carries even more weight with most people. This is why politicians give speeches instead of only handouts; why so many colleges and universities require students to be present at lectures, even when a professor's book is more detailed and interesting; and why the legal systems of many countries insist that live witnesses give verbal testimony instead of, or in addition to, written reports. Of course, there may be economic factors as well, but the authority of the spoken word is of paramount importance in every human society.

43

In spite of the fact that people give tremendous authority to the words of those they think of as important, the spoken and mental words that individuals use in their daily lives have the greatest impact on their own bodies and minds, especially when these words reinforce beliefs, habits, and expectations. Even if a powerful authority figure says something very impressive, it does not take full effect until the listener has agreed to it, repeated it several times to himself or herself, either aloud or silently, and has recreated it in memory several times while reinforcing it with emotion and/or behavior. In fact, I would go so far as to say that all real authority comes from within, for we are the ones who give authority to someone or something, and we are the ones who deny it or take it away.

Word Choices

In choosing the words to use with the Dynamind Technique I was guided by the desire to make the strongest possible impression on the subconscious in the least possible amount of time. In order to do this I had to consider a number of different verbal styles and factors.

The Affirmative Style. In this style of speaking a person expresses a positive idea in the form of statement of fact, such as "I am healthy," or "I am happy." If the statement is indeed factual, that is, if it reinforces something the person knows to be true, then it can have an immediate, positive effect. If however, if the statement affirms something the person wishes were true, like saying "I am healthy" when you are sick, or "I am happy" when you are sad, then the actual condition greatly diminishes the effect of the affirmation.

One way around this limitation is to use repetition. If you repeat an affirmative statement often enough, then resistance to the idea grows less and acceptance increases. In one of my classes I have the whole group affirm "I am feeling good" nonstop for one minute, and at the end of that time everyone is feeling better than when they started. Of course, in this case the group reinforcement is an important part of the relatively quick response, as is the fact that almost everyone in the group is feeling somewhat good to begin with. When a person is feeling bad and doing the process by oneself, it generally takes a lot more repetition to get the full effect, sometimes hours, days, weeks or more.

Another way around the limitation of affirming something that is not true right now is to use enthusiastic emotion. Strong emotion carries a lot of authority, and the subconscious responds to it very well. If a person who is not healthy could say, "I am healthy!" with enough positive emotional force behind it, he or she would probably get a good response in a very short time. Unfortunately, very few people seem able to generate that kind of emotion at will, and even if one could do it, there are not many places where it would be socially acceptable or convenient.

A third way is to phrase the affirmation in such a way as to diminish the conflict with a current condition. Some people will shift the intention into the future with a statement like "I can be healthy," or "I will be happy," but this almost always brings up the necessity for extended repetition. Gary Craig, who inspired me with his Emotional Freedom Technique, came up with an excellent solution with his conditional phrase, "Even though..." that precedes an affirmation. So one might say, "Even though I'm not healthy, I love myself unconditionally." It works amazingly well, and yet there are too many conditions and situations for which it is either not appropriate or not acceptable to the person using it.

The Request Style. This takes the form of "Please do this for me." Regardless of who or what is being asked to do it, this is placing the power to heal or to change outside of oneself. I decided not to use this form because it sounds too much like what is commonly called prayer, and also because my purpose is to strengthen internal authority, and not to diminish it.

The Command Style. This style might work for very assertive people who are used to being obeyed when they give orders. If for any reason your body dared not to be healthy or happy, you would simply issue the command, "Get well!" or "Feel happy!" With sufficient emotional force and expectation of results you would probably get very fast results. The limitation is that not enough people are assertive enough to make it usable on a broad scale.

A variation on Command is the "Direction Style." Instead of issuing a military-type order, you give a directing type of order the way you would when ordering from a menu in a restaurant. Therefore, all you would have to is use the same tone of voice and state of expectation when saying, "Bring me the special of the day and a cup of coffee" as you would when saying, "Lower my blood pressure and relax my shoulders." The main difficulty that I found with this style is that it requires a calm, confident state of expectation with no concern about who is taking the order, a requirement that is often hard to meet when you are suffering from painful symptoms of various kinds.

The Dynamind Style. Practically speaking, any words of any kind that work for you are the best ones to use. Nevertheless, my years of teaching have demonstrated to me that when learning a new technique, as for painting, cooking, or healing, it helps tremendously to begin with a standard system, recipe, or process. After you become confident enough in applying the standard you can, if you choose, create your own variations on it.

For that reason, I developed a standard statement for use with Dynamind. Although I call this a "Direction" or a "Declaration" in some of my writings, it is really a short phrase that combines three different affirmations of the first type I mentioned: the affirmation that reinforces an existing fact. Here is the Basic Form of the Statement used for most Dynamind work:

"I have a problem and that can change;

I want the problem to go away."

Let's examine each of the three parts that I mentioned above.

The first part, "I have a problem," acknowledges the existing condition or situation. In addition to affirming what is, the act of consciously acknowledging it very often begins a process of relaxation because it lowers resistance to the fact of its existence.

The second part, "...and that can change," affirms the fact that anything can change, because everything does change. By not setting a deadline, and yet still creating a sense of expectation, this part of the statement tends to produce even more relaxation.

The third part, "I want the problem to go away," affirms what I have found to be the most universally consistent motivation among all the clients and students I have worked with around the world. If someone has a decidedly different motivation, it can be substituted here, but this one will work for most people most of the time.

This Basic Statement has proven its effectiveness in thousands of cases in various countries. In the rest of the book you will find many examples of effective word substitutions for specific purposes, but don't discount the power of the Basic form. It is simple enough to memorize easily, which will make it easier for you to insert different words of your choice when that seems the right thing to do, and to be sure of what to say when you can't think of anything else. I once did a two-day workshop covering physical, emotional and mental problems, and this was the only wording I used – successfully – for every demonstration case.

On The Use Of Touch

You may be familiar with the fact that you have organs inside your body, like your liver, kidneys, and stomach, but you may not be aware that the skin that covers your whole body is also considered to be an organ. In addition to keeping most of your other organs from falling out, it also serves as one of your most important sources of sensory input from the world around you, as a means of eliminating toxins from other organs and cells, as a way of taking in nutrients, as an internal and external medium of communication, and much, much more.

One of the most interesting and useful characteristics of this remarkable organ has to do with the fact that when the skin is stimulated in various ways a beneficial result can be noted inside the body, sometimes at a location quite distant from the site of stimulation. The same sorts of stimulation may also produce beneficial emotional and mental changes as well.

According to available sources this knowledge of the relationship between skin stimulation and healing has been put to practical use since very ancient times. Massage therapy of some sort has been, and still is, part of the healing repertoire of many cultures around the world. Bas-reliefs at the Temple of Physicians in Egypt apparently demonstrate the use of foot and body massage, and there is no question about the antiquity of China's famous system of acupuncture.

In modern times it has been shown that virtually any kind of gentle skin stimulation will produce an endorphin response, but a number of systems of healing touch put most of the emphasis on the stimulation of certain specific points on the skin for the purpose of inducing more specific responses.

Of course, the most well-known and elaborate system of this type comes from China, where they have designated as many as eight hundred different points on the body arranged along pathways called "meridians," and accompanied by a complex body of philosophy and theory. In practice, these points are stimulated by a wide variety of methods, including needles of varying sizes and materials that are twirled or left in place; burning herbs that are placed directly on the skin or at the upper ends of the needles; localized massage or finger pressure, sometimes with the addition of essential oils or medical salves; subcutaneous injection of medicine in liquid form; and even surgical incision for the placement of objects such as gold beads to maintain stimulation over a long period of time. In more modern times there has been the addition of vibration, electrical currents, magnetic fields, and laser beams. "Psychic energy," whether projected from the hands or the mind alone is also used at the acupuncture points, but it is not clear if that is an ancient or a modern practice.

While some other cultures have applied crystals, ointments, and amulets to specific points on the skin, most of those that recognize such points rely predominantly on direct touch, either with deep pressure or light contact. Significantly, Chinese culture seems to be the only one to have developed the meridian concept as it is used in China, but all cultures who use the skin itself for healing seem to agree that there are specific points that produce specific results.

I was first introduced to "touch healing" by my Hawaiian aunt in the late 1950s. She taught me a system of light touch therapy that I have called "Kahi Loa," and which is described in detail in my book, *Instant Healing*. As part of that system I learned about fourteen important healing points used in her tradition: the crown of the head, the ends of the shoulders, center of the palms; the center of the chest, the navel, the pubic bone, the seventh cervical vertebra, the coccyx, the hips, and the center of the soles of the feet. In Old Hawaii, and to some extent today, these points, as well as any sore points on the body, are stimulated by pressure with a "lomi stick," a kind of hooked, wooden rod, or by hand or fingers. However, I also learned to stimulate them by light rubbing, brushing, holding with an energetic focus, and even by moving the "aka field" or "aura" above them.

At the University of Colorado in the early 1960s while majoring in Chinese Studies, I learned about acupuncture and began practicing with several types of acupressure, such as Do-In and Jin Shin Do. During my seven years in Africa I learned how to apply crystals and herbs to specific parts of the body, and after I returned to the USA in 1971 I studied and practiced the point systems of Reflexology, Applied Kinesiology, and Self-Therap/Ease.

When it came time to develop the Dynamind Technique I knew I wanted to include a touch component, but for a while I suffered from "knowledge overload" as a result of being familiar with too many systems and theories. Finally, I simply defined the criteria that I wanted:

1. No more than four points so they would be easy to remember.
2. One point for the front of the body, one for each side, and one for the back.
3. Each point had to be easy to reach for most people under most conditions.
4. Each point had to have significant benefits in its own right.

The next thing I did was to experiment with points

that I knew were significant, and that experts in the field also considered significant. By significant, I mean that the point reveals stress by feeling tender under pressure and, for most people, stimulation of the point produces significant physiological changes, including tingling, current sensations, relaxation of tension, and/or an increase in well-being. Eventually, I decided on the following four points:

A. The so-called "Thymus Point" in the center of the chest, not associated with any acupuncture point, but developed and used very effectively by Dr. John Diamond, a medical doctor who has worked with many holistic therapies, including applied kinesiology. As a means of balancing or harmonizing the energy of the body he taught people how to stimulate the area of the thymus gland by a light, rapid tapping with the fingers. My own experiments demonstrated that this simple technique was very effective in producing physical relaxation, emotional calming, and mental clarity.

B. There is an acupuncture point on each hand located at the juncture where the bones of the forefinger and thumb meet. If you feel around in that area with the thumb of your opposite hand you will find a small indentation or hollow that, if you are stressed, may hurt quite a bit when you press it. This point is called "Hoku" in Chinese, and although it is most well known for use with headaches and insomnia, some acupuncture experts use it as a primary point for many ailments. The October-December 1981 issue of the American Journal of Acupuncture notes that the Hoku point can "have powerful effects on the autonomic nervous system," and recommends gentle stimulation. My experiments indicate that it has similar effects to the Thymus Point described above.

C. For the fourth point, if you count each hand as having one point, I chose the seventh cervical vertebra, designated as C7 in modern terms and *hokua* in Hawaiian. For practical purposes it is the raised part of the backbone at the base of the neck, or the top of the spine. Although I have been unable to find any therapuetic use of this point in modern medical literature, my Hawaiian aunt told me repeatedly how important it was. My own observations have indicated that it is a major stress point, meaning that is a place on the body, just like the others described above, where stress tends to accumulate. The condition known as "widow's hump" or "dowager's hump," which occurs in this area, is associated with osteoporosis, but by working with stress/ tension reduction techniques I have been able to reduce or eliminate this condition in several clients, including my mother. My experiments with gentle stimulation of this area are similar to those mentioned above with Hoku.

After deciding which points to use I had to design a way to use them. Here is where my experience with Kahi Loa came in very handy. The seventh step in Kahi Loa, called "Kahi Kanaka," involves lightly touching certain points on the body in a specific sequence, starting with the top of the head and ending with the feet. My aunt emphasized the importance of maintaining the touch on each point just long enough for it to be definitely felt, and just short enough for the next point to feel connected to the point that preceded it. It took me awhile to realize, and personally experience, that this kind of timed sequencing helped to make the body feel whole. When you touch the body gently in different places, lingering for about three to five seconds at each place, the body remembers the sensation during the next several touches. The result of this process is to create a sense of connectedness, which helps to relieve stress and increase relaxation. The same effect could be achieved by one other person massaging you all over with a gentle caress, or by several people gently holding their hands on several parts of your body at the same time, but for a technique designed to help you help yourself it has to be done a little differently.

Therefore, in the touch segment of Dynamind I settled on a sequence of touching the chosen points for a duration of seven counts in this order: chest, hand, hand, neck. It doesn't matter which hand you touch first and, in fact, it really doesn't matter what sequence you use, but for learning purposes the above sequence is very good. If the back of the neck cannot be reached for any reason, then the touch of the chest point can be repeated. There is nothing special about the number seven, except that it is a good rhythm that is easy to remember and most people I have worked with do the count in three to five seconds.

Types Of Touch

For centuries, acupuncture and other special point therapies have used virtually every possible form of touch for stimulating the points they treat. I have experimented with many of these forms and have found them to be about equally effective in producing beneficial physical, emotional and mental changes. Here are the ones most commonly applied in Dynamind.

Tapping. This is very popular with the more modern

"energy" therapies such as the Callahan Method and Gary Craig's Emotional Freedom Technique. It is usually the first type taught to students and clients of Dynamind, because it has the advantage of being physically and psychologically impressive. It also looks good on stage for a workshop demonstration. Some first-time users try to literally pound the points with a fist or a hand, but it is much more effective to tap lightly with two or three fingers.

Holding. Simply holding the points with several fingers works just as well as tapping. Strong pressure is not necessary, but the touch needs to be firm enough to bring conscious attention to the point being touched. A somewhat greater effect is obtained by holding and humming at the same time. It is even more effective to hold an object like "The Amazing Managizer," "The Huna Power Coin," or a favorite crystal on each point for the count of seven.

Vibrating and Brushing. As a simple variation preferred by some people, you can hold the point and vibrate or shake the skin above it back and forth, or you can lightly brush the point with the tips of your fingers.

Mental Focus. There may be times when you want to use the Dynamind Technique, but circumstances make it very awkward or impossible to do so. This could be while driving a car, waiting in line, attending a meeting or a party, or many other situations. In this case you can touch the points mentally in your preferred way. To be effective, you must be able to imagine the touch being as realistic as possible, so I recommend that you use this type only after some practice with a more physical touch. By this means your mental focus can stimulate the memory of real touch, and that will stimulate the points effectively.

On The Use Of Breath

Nearly everyone takes breathing for granted unless

something interferes with it. This is because in humans the process of breathing is governed by the autonomic nervous system, which simply means that breathing is automatic. Something inside us takes care of breathing while our conscious self plays games, talks to people, and does all the "important" stuff of life. In that sense we are better off than the dolpins, who have only voluntary control of their breathing. The poor things can't even get a good night's sleep because part of their brain has to stay awake to keep on breathing.

Breathing is the single most important thing we do to stay alive, because we do not live very long without doing it. We can go weeks without food, days without water, but only minutes without air. Practically everyone knows that we breath to supply our cells with oxygen for burning the fuel we need for energy, but fewer people know that breathing is the major pump for our lymph system and one of the most important means by which we eliminate toxins. Unfortunately, stress responses tend to produce shallow breathing, which can greatly reduce all the benefits of breathing.

Although breathing is automatic for us humans, we also have the option of voluntary control if we want to use it. So we can consciously train ourselves to breath in special ways that benefit our bodies, our feelings, and our minds, such as holding our breath under water for extended periods, breathing more deeply to improve our health, controlling our breath for speaking and singing, using our breath to calm our emotions and thoughts, and much, much more. For instance, in my library I have a book by Yogi Ramacharaka called *The Science of Breath* that a contains wealth of techniques for using the breath to gain spiritual powers and knowledge.

In the Hawaiian language there is a single word, *ha*, that means "breath, life, spirit," and "to breath upon something to give it life or to make it sacred." In former times sacred breathing was always used for important rituals.

I have studied breathing techniques from around the world, but I mostly use one that my Hawaiian uncle taught me, called piko-piko. Essentially, it consists of consciously inhaling while you hold your attention on one thing, and consciously exhaling while you hold your attention on a different thing. Theoretically, this produces a wave of energy between the two points. Pikopiko has many variations and I have written extensively about it elsewhere, so here I will only say that I chose a form of it for the Dynamind Technique that is highly effective for relieving stress and energizing body and mind at the same time. It is the last step in the Dynamind Technique, and DMT is not as effective without it.

1. After finishing the Touch sequence, inhale with your attention on the top of your head. If you have trouble putting or keeping your attention on that spot, you can help yourself focus by imagining a light or an object there, or even by touching the area with a finger. You only need to keep your attention there for the length of the inhale, but you can maintain it with a count of seven if you choose.

2. After the inhale, exhale with your attention on your feet or your toes. You do not need to visualize or imagine energy moving through your body down to your toes, because the energy automatically follows your shift of attention. Of course, if it makes you feel better to do that, then go right ahead. A slight movement of your toes will be all that you will need to help you move your attention. One complete breath is sufficient for one round of Dynamind, but don't let that

stop you from continuing to breathe as much as you want.

On The Use Of Symbols

One of the most fascinating areas of research and practice related to health and healing has to do with the use of symbols to communicate directly with your subconscious, your body, or your autonomic nervous system (pick the words you like best). Here I am not concerned with external symbols like Hindu yantras or the Hawaiian Eye of Kanaloa. What is even more fascinating to my mind are the self-generated internal symbols that can have such a profound influence on body, mind and, perhaps, even circumstances.

In her book, *Imagery in Healing*, Dr. Jeanne Achterberg writes:

> "A profound relationship exists between the brain, behavior, psychological factors, and the immune system, although the exact nature of the relationship has yet to be specified. New behavioral therapies that highlight the imagination, such as guided imagery, hypnosis, biofeedback – all with a distinct tinge of shamanism – have been shown to influence immunology under controlled testing situations."

In other words, we can consciously use imaginary symbols to assist the body in healing itself, but we don't know how it works. This is very upsetting to those who want to keep the mind and body separate, but very useful to those who are more interested in results.

My shamanic training with my father began with symbol work, and I have used inner symbols for healing with great success for more than fifty years, so it was natural that I would want to incorporate symbols into the Dynamind Technique.

My first version of Dynamind did, in fact, use a symbol right at the beginning. At that time every round began with imagining a refreshing waterfall, and it was quite well received. I also used symbols in addition to, or instead of, the verbal Statement. However, in the process of reducing the process of Dynamind to its most effective minimum, I discovered that the waterfall image in the beginning was nice, but not necessary, and that in most cases the imagery during the round was not necessary, either.

Nevertheless, in some cases, imagery is vital to the effectiveness of the technique. The main problem is that many people are not able to come up with an appropriate image on their own and, after all, Dynamind is intended to be first and foremost a self-healing technique.

In the following chapters I will give many examples of how imagery was used in specific cases. Such images are called "Symkeys" because they act like keys for unlocking tension. Here and now I will present a simple formula for generating a healing image that nearly anyone can use.

Structurally, when a image is used in Dynamind it comes right after the Statement and before the Touch, or, if desired, it is incorporated into the Statement itself. To increase the effectiveness of the image you can describe it to yourself in words as you create it and use it.

1. Ask yourself, "If this symptom had a shape, what would it be?" Then name the first shape that comes to mind.
2. Ask yourself, "If this symptom had a color, what would it be?" Then name the first color that comes to mind.
3. Ask yourself, "If this symptom had a weight, what would it be?" Then name the first weight that comes to mind.

4. Now imagine that an invisible friend, angel, or other helper is reaching into your body and removing this symbol with its specific shape, color, and weight. Do this three times with as much detail as possible, and then proceed with the rest of the Dynamind Technique.

The Intensity Scale

Over the years I have used various ways of subjectively measuring the results of healing techniques, but I wish to give credit to Gary Craig for inspiring me to use a variation of his scale with Dynamind. Such a scale is of more use to therapists and workshop demonstrations than it is to individuals using the technique on their own, but it can help you to be aware of changes from round to round.

1. Pick a number from 0 to 10 to represent the intensity of the problem before you begin the Dynamind Technique. In this case, 0 represents no problem, and 10 represents a severe problem.

2. After each round, pick a number again to represent the current state of the problem. Remember, a small change is still a change.

3. Continue doing rounds, using variations as appropriate, until the number is 1 or 0, until no change occurs no matter what you do, or until you want to stop.

Guidelines For Practice

Here are a few things that can help you make better use of the Dynamind Technique. Some of them will be discussed in later chapters as well in the context of specific examples.

1. Keep doing rounds of Dynamind until you

get all the relief you want or have time for. Sometimes a specific symptom needs several rounds to relieve all the tension, or the relief of one symptom uncovers a different symptom.

2.   Whenever possible, use specific sensations or feelings in describing the problem, not abstract labels. "I have a cold" is abstract. "I have a stuffy nose" is specific. "I am angry" is alright, but "I feel anger in my solar plexus" is better.

3.   If a pain or other symptom seems to change location after one or more rounds of Dynamind, assume that the new location represents a different symptom on a different stress layer, whether the symptom on the new layer is of the same type as the first one or not. For example, a Dynamind session might start with a pain in the chest on the first round, change to a pain in the shoulder on the second round, and trembling in the legs on the next round.

4.   If a physical symptom does not change at all after three rounds of Dynamind, assume that a suppressed emotion is involved, even if you are not aware of one. When no emotional connection is apparent, try anger first, then fear. Use Statements like "There may be anger in my shoulder," or "My eyes may be afraid of something." If there is some relief, keep using the emotional assumption until the symptom is gone or it is no longer helpful.

5.   If neither the physical approach nor the emotional assumption provide relief, or when you have done as much as you can with them and the problem persists, incorporate imagery into the process.

6. To help invalids, very young children, animals, or anyone else who cannot do the Dynamind Technique on their own, touch, hug, or caress the subject in a way that will establish emotional rapport. This will take the place of the Gesture. Then, while still keeping physical contact, make a Statement on behalf of the subject, using the form "Blank has a problem..." Next, do the Touch segment with your hands or fingers, and touch the top of the subject's head and the base of the spine as you do the Breath, making allowances for the position, condition, and anatomy of the subject.

7. When you find yourself in circumstances where doing Dynamind in the normal way might be embarrassing or inconvenient, such as while in an office or while driving a car, you can do the whole process mentally, without gesturing, speaking out loud, or touching the points physically. It helps a great deal to have done the process normally a few times in order to create memories that you can use for focusing.

8. As a therapist or just a friend, you can help someone to use Dynamind without even knowing what the problem is. The client can simply think of the specific problem, with or without speaking the Basic Statement out loud, while you guide the person through the steps of the process. This is very useful when someone is too embarrassed or otherwise reluctant to make the problem known to someone else. The session will end when the person wants to stop.

9. If Dynamind does not help at all, use something else or combine Dynamind with another

approach. What Dynamind does best is to relieve tension. It does not cure anything. If relieving tension is not sufficient or appropriate for helping with your problem, then the best thing you can do is to do something different or to get some help.

Statement Variations

Feeling Statements. I have already said that the particular words used in the Statement can be modified to suit the circumstances and the individual. A class of phrases I call "Feeling Statements" is one of the most beneficial modifications you can make. The effectiveness of the Dynamind Technique is greatly enhanced by relating any condition to a specific physical sensation, and these phrases help to do that very well. Some examples are:

"I feel pain in the third joint of my little finger…"

"I feel anxiety in my chest…"

"I feel anger in my stomach…"

"I feel an urge to eat when I watch television…"

When using a Feeling Statement the motivation becomes "I want that feeling to go away."

Thinking Statements. These are exceptionally useful for issues dealing with the past or the future or the expanded present. The dwelling on problems remembered from the past, anticipated in the future, or existing out of sight always produces tension in the present moment. When that tension is relieved the problems either disappear or the reaction to them changes enough so that they can be more easily resolved. Examples of this kind of statement are:

"When I think of what happened I feel…"

"When I think of flying in a plane I feel…"

"When I think of the work on my desk I feel…"

Basic Extensions. Again I emphasize that the best

words are the ones that work. When you still aren't sure which ones to use, then a simple extension of the first or last parts of the Basic Statement may help a great deal. Example:

"I have a problem with my right knee,... I want that problem to go away and be replaced by good feeling and flexibility."

Power Statements. These are statements that resemble affirmations and that are intended to reinforce or establish positive behavior, rather than to resolve a problem. Here, the combination of statement, touch, and breath serves to strengthen the idea being presented. They are most effective when applied after using Dynamind to resolve any related physical, mental, or emotional issues because they are accepted and remembered by the subconscious mind more readily if related tension is less or absent. Examples:

"I have the power to speak in front of people without getting nervous, yes I do. Make it happen, make it so!"

"My body knows how to get rid of my excess fat, yes it does, and my body is starting to do that now!"

The Dynamind Toner. This form is a non-specific variation intended for general stress relief and reinforcement of positive qualities. It uses emotional and mental assumptions followed by a generalized power statement. In doing the Toner you use the Gesture, Statement, Touch and Breath for each numbered segment. Here is one version:

1. "There may be fear, anxiety, worry or doubt in my body and my mind, and that can change. I want all those problems to go away."
2. "There may be anger, resentment, unhappiness or guilt in my body and my mind, and that can change. I want all those problems to go away."

3. "There is love and peace, harmony and happiness somewhere in my body and my mind, and that is good. I want those feelings to grow and spread."

4. "There is power and strength, health and vitality somewhere in my body and my mind, and that is good. I want those qualities to grow and spread."

Feel free to change the wording according to your needs and desires. This is very good for beginning and ending the day.

Dynamind In Action

The chapters to follow will include many case examples of how Dynamind has worked in actual situations all over the world. These will be presented in three different forms: Workshop Demonstrations, Client Sessions, and Informal Anecdotes.

The cases in each chapter have been given a numerical sequence, along with a code that designates the chapter content and the source of the case. Any of my cases will contain the letters "SK." Certified Dynamind Practitioner cases, which comprise the majority of the examples, will have a neutral letter code, and informal anecdotes will be designated by an "X." Case reports have been edited only where necessary to further protect the privacy of practitioners, clients, subjects, and those who have voluntarily shared their experiences.

Workshop Demonstrations. Whenever I give a workshop on the Dynamind Technique I include a number of stage demonstrations for using it with pain, emotional problems, and other issues. These demonstrations usually take one to two minutes, with a few taking as long as five minutes. Even though the time period is very short, we often get complete relief from the problem presented, but just about as often we finish the demonstration with partial relief and the subject is advised to continue the process independently. Sometimes there are follow-up results during or after the workshop and sometimes there are not.

To do the demonstrations I ask for a volunteer from the audience. This person comes up on the stage and I guide him or her through the process in a standing position. We may simply use the Basic Formula Statement, but more often we use the words provided by the subject and incorporate them into the Basic Format. In some cases I might suggest a wording, but I always ask for the subject's approval. On occasion I might use imagery if it seems appropriate. Tapping is used for nearly every demonstration because it is a good visual aid for the audience, although I may use another form of touch to show the possible variations.

Client Sessions. These are more fully documented cases recorded by myself or by those whom I have trained as Certified Practitioners.

Anyone may use the Dynamind Technique privately or as part of a therapeutic practice without any restrictions. However, I have developed a mentoring program for those who wish to develop their skill in using Dynamind, and who wish to be on a referral list. After providing a certain number of case studies in a specified format, each of which I comment on, these people are granted a certificate as a Dynamind Practitioner. For details on this program see the Appendix.

All of the client session case studies used in this book come from myself or from the Certified Practitioners. The formal case study format provides certain information about the case, but a good degree of flexibility is allowed because of the widely varying backgrounds of the Practitioners and the sometimes very different uses to which they put the process. In general, though, the cases include the sex and age of the client, the presenting problem, the intensity if a scale is used, the type of Statement, a description of imagery if it is used, the results of each round, and the final resolution of the session.

Dynamind is intended to be applied by the person with the problem. In most cases, therefore, the Practitioner explains the technique first, then guides the client through the process, making suggestions for variations as appropriate. In some cases the physical or mental condition of the client is such that the Practitioner speaks the words and does the touching for the client, and in other cases involving more unusual applications of the process the Practitioner applies the technique mentally.

Client sessions are not always done in an office. Because the Dynamind Technique is so simple and can be learned so rapidly, sessions may take place in a restaurant, in an airport, over the phone, or in any other location.

The Dynamind Technique is amazing by itself, and it is also an amazingly useful complement to other techniques or healing modalities. For this reason, some of the Practitioners incorporate Dynamind into another therapeutic approach, or incorporate other forms of therapy into Dynamind. This may bring up questions as to how much of a healing effect was brought about by Dynamind, but my interest is in helping to heal the client by whatever healthy means possible, not in deciding where to place the credit. The answer to that is simple: healing always comes from within. The client (or user) is the healer. The Dynamind Technique, and any other healing techniques, are, in the final analysis, only tools. The most important aspect of healing is the healing itself, not the method.

Informal Anecdotes. Most of these come by email or letter from people who have used the Technique on themselves, or who have shared it with a friend or family member. Certain kinds of case studies by Practitioners in which feedback results are probable, but not verifiable, will also fall into this category. Usually there is not much information provided about the specific process used, so I will only refer to this type of case when it is especially interesting, or, as you will see, when it deserves a chapter of its own.

Glossary

In some of the case studies you may encounter words or phrases that are not self-explanatory. I will explain them in this section.

The Dynamind Destresser. This is simply a term that I have used in some workshops for the Basic Form of the Dynamind Technique.

The Dynamind Developer. This is a name sometimes given to a Dynamind process using Power Statements.

The Emlock. A short-hand term for "Emotional Lock." This term describes a situation when, during one or more rounds of Dynamind, emotional tension cannot be relieved by words alone.

The Symkey. A short-hand term for a "Symbolic Key" used to open an "Emotional Lock." Originally, I employed a standard image of a locked door and had the client imagine inserting a key and opening the door before proceeding with the tapping. It worked quite well for a lot of people, but I dropped it as a standard for the sake of more creative imagery that allows much greater flexibility in releasing the tension of complex emotional tangles. Now any imagery may be called a Symkey.

Emotional Assumption. Normally, when working with a physical symptom the application of the Dynamind Technique begins with a Statement that refers directly to that symptom. For instance, if you have a headache you say "I have a headache and that can change, etc." While this produces good results in the majority of cases, it often happens that this only gives partial relief, or perhaps none at all. In this case I have found it extremely useful to assume the presence of an emotional lock, even though the client may not be aware of any emotional content related to the symptom.

As a general rule I recommend assuming the presence of anger first, and then, depending on the results, fear next, unless I'm pretty sure of which one to use in the beginning. So, a statement assuming the presence of anger would take the form of "There may be anger in my head" or "My head is angry about something, etc.," followed by the touch and the breath. Perhaps surprisingly, this approach can be very effective in relieving more layers of tension.

Dynamind can help most people with most problems most of the time, but not all people with all problems all of the time. The next chapters will help you to use it for the greatest positive effect.

Chapter Three
RELIEVING PAIN

Pain is the most common human complaint in the whole, wide world. Everyone knows what it feels like, yet no one knows what it is.

Does that surprise you? One would think that modern science would know what causes pain, but during my research on the subject I came across the opinions of many medical doctors who say that our present knowledge of pain physiology is "primitive" or "rudimentary."

That hasn't stopped people from coming up with numerous theories, though. Pain is such an important topic that it will be worthwhile to find out what various people have thought about it in the past, and what they think about it now.

Pain Theories

Immediately we confront the problem of defining just what pain is. The International Association for the Study of Pain defines it as "an unpleasant sensory and emotional experience associated with actual or potential tissue damage, or described in terms of such damage." Interesting, but I know of many pain experiences that don't have any relationship to actual or potential tissue damage, and that are not even described in terms of such damage. Headaches are one example, menstrual cramps are another, and I'm sure you could find more examples on your own. Webster's

Encyclopedic Unabridged Dictionary of the English Language defines it as "a distressing sensation in a particular part of the body." That is more clear, but "a distressing sensation" doesn't quite describe the pain experience, so I'll use one of my own: "Pain is the subjective experience that something hurts." Now let's look at some of the theories of how it happens.

The Specificity Theory. This one is very old, but it lasted a long time. First proposed by the Greek Epicurus in the third century B.C. (as far as we know), it stated that pain was directly equated with injury, and left psychological factors out of the equation. In 1644 the philosopher René Descartes thought that there was a substance known at the time as "phlogiston" which was liberated during the combustion of fire, and that when a person felt pain on being burned it was because the phlogiston from the fire caused a spot on the skin to move, thus pulling on some kind of thread in the body that led to the brain which produced the pain sensation. He likened it to pulling on a rope in the basement of a church to make the bell ring in the belfry. As regards pain from other injuries he thought that the intensity of pain was directly related to the amount of associated injury, just like Epicurus. The theory makes sense when it is applied to simple injuries, but it cannot explain many other kinds of pain, especially chronic pain that continues even after an injury has healed.

A Dr. Von Frey in 1894 proposed a solution by saying that the human skin has sensory points for touch, warmth, cold and pain, and that free nerve endings were specific receptors for pain. In a similar way to Descartes he thought that there was a sort of direct nerve line from the injury site to the brain. Unfortunately for the theory, clinical and physiological evidence didn't support the concept. The most serious challenge to the Specificity Theory came from

Dr. Henry Beecher who treated inujured soldiers from Anzio during the Second World War. He noted that only one out of five soldiers brought into the hospital required morphine to reduce their pain level. On the other hand, when treating civilian patients with similar wounds after the war, he found that the civilians were much more likely to require morphine to control the pain. Dr. Beecher's conclusion was that there was no direct relationship between the intensity of the pain and the severity of the wound. In fact, he decided that the emotional state of the patient influenced the level of pain more than the injury itself.

The Gate Control Theory. There are at least a dozen other theories about pain, including the Reverberating Circuits Theory, the Two Pathway Theory, The Aspect Theory, and the Endogenous Opiate Theory, but the most popular one today among physicians around the world is the Gate Control Theory, developed in the early 1960s by Drs. Ronald Melzack and Patrick Wall. As Dr. William Deardorff put it in 2003, "It's scientific beauty is that it provides a physiological basis for the complex phenomenon of pain." However, another doctor has said that "The greatest weakness of the theory is that it is still largely a physiological model." That means it does not adequately cover psychological aspects of the phenomenon of pain.

In extremely simple terms, the Gate Control Theory supposes that there is some kind of "nerve gate" within the bundle of nerves at the base of the spine that regulates the flow of pain messages to the brain. Basically, injuries and negative emotions or attitudes open the gate, and pain relief treatments or positive emotions or attitudes close the gate. Allowance is also made for "signals from the brain" to modify the opening or closing, but the nature of these signals is very unclear from the material I have read.

In my view this theory fails to take into account the

very real experiences of emotional and mental pain, as well as pain that can occur without any physical injury. Also, there does not seem to be any explanation for the simultaneous experience of both pain and pleasure, which most people have felt at one time or another. As Dr. Deardorff has observed, "No one yet understands the details of this process or how to control it."

The Oxygen Deprivation Theory. Dr. Majid Ali, Professor of Medicine at the Capital University of Integrative Medicine in Washington, D.C., has developed a theory of pain particularly in relation to the disease of fibromyalgia. The official name of his theory is Oxidative-Dysoxygenative Dysfunction (ODD), and is based on a concept of of a problem with oxygen metabolism in the cells. He presents what he calls three basic facts about fibromyalgia as follows:

1. All symptoms of fibromyalgia are caused by cellular oxygen deprivation.
2. Oxygen deprivation is caused by dysfunctional oxygen metabolism.
3. Oxygen metabolism becomes abnormal due to excessive and cumulative oxidative stress caused by sugar overload, antibiotic abuse, undiagnosed allergies, synthetic chemicals, and anger.

Although his concentration is on fibromyalgia, Dr. Ali considers many other symptoms besides pain to be due to oxygen deprivation.

The Sarno Theory. Based on twenty-four years of successfully treating what he calls Tension Myositis Syndrome (TMS), Dr. John Sarno, Professor of Rehabilitation Medicine at the New York University School of Medicine, theorizes a mind-body connection based on the idea that emotionally-induced tension is the major cause of most of the pain that people experience, as well as being the factor behind many other common physical disturbances. In his book, *Healing*

Back Pain, he says that he pursued this idea after too many unsuccessful uses of back surgery to stop pain. Among his unorthodox forms of treatment is lecturing people who have back pain on why they don't have to have it, and he reports impressive success with this approach.

I had occasion to try out Dr. Sarno's theory when I was working on a project to clear trees and brush from an ancient Hawaiian temple on Kauai. Part of my task involved lifting cut logs about six inches (15 cm) in diameter and throwing them over a wall. After forty-five minutes of this under a hot sun with no break and no water, I suddenly got a sharp pain in the lumbar region of my back. "Common sense" would have blamed the physical stress of lifting and dehydration as the reasons for the pain, but I decided to experiment anyway. Assuming that my body/subconscious just didn't want to do what I was doing any more, I remained bent over and spent five minutes telling my body that bending was normal, that it was designed to bend, that it was okay to keep lifting, and that we would take a break later. By that time the pain was all gone and I continued tossing logs for another hour without any problem before stopping for a rest. On another occasion I used a similar process to permanently get rid of an onset of carpal tunnel syndrome during a long session at my computer.

While Dr. Sarno's theory makes sense in its own context, and his treatments do work, I think that for many cases they take longer than necessary.

The Dynamind Theory. One of the big problems with all of the above theories is that they are unable to explain the kinds of pain relief that we get with the Dynamind Technique. I am not a medical doctor, nor am I an expert in physiology. However, I am a reasonably intelligent human being and I know how to theorize as well as the next person. My theory is simple, practical, and based on thirty years of

73

helping people to get rid of their own pain. Keep in mind that what I am about to say is not necessarily true. Like all of the above theories, it, too, is just a theory. My Dynamind Theory of Pain (DTP) goes like this:

1. Resisting experience causes tension in the body.
2. Excessive tension causes pain and other problems in the body and in the mind.
3. Relieve the tension and the pain disappears and the problems heal themselves.

Please note that this theory doesn't say how the tension has to be relieved. Nor does it say how the pain occurs. All it says is that if you relieve the tension, then the pain will go away. You could use meditation or you could use surgery, it really doesn't matter as long as they end up relieving more tension than they cause.

As far as how the pain occurs, I am personally inclined toward a combined version of the theories of Ali and Sarno. If pain is actually a signal of oxygen deprivation, and if tension really is a dominant factor in most, if not all, illness, then it seems eminently logical that tension is the source of the oxygen deprivation at the cell level. It could be a direct source when it interferes directly with oxygen supply, as when tension inhibits blood flow, and an indirect source when it affects an organ or function that interferes with oxygen metabolism. What I like about this idea is that it offers a logical basis for the experience that reducing tension promotes healing. However, it is still just a theory.

Of course, this book is about the Dynamind Technique, so let's finally take a look at how well this method relieves pain. Even when the Touch and the Breath are not mentioned in a case study, by the way, they are always used.

Quick and Easy Pain Relief

Pain is the most common complaint that people

have, and therefore most of our case studies are concerned with it. And the majority of those are about pain relief after three rounds of Dynamind. Considering that one round of Dynamind takes about thirty seconds, this means relief in about one minute and a half or less. Not all cases are about pain relief in this short a time by any means. Some sessions require many more rounds, some cases require more than one session, and with some cases the full relief does not occur until after the session is over. Here, nevertheless, is a sampling of short cases. Take note of the different kinds of pain that were successfully treated in this way.

Case PSK01–Neck pain: This is a case from a workshop demonstration. The subject was a woman who had suffered chronic pain in her neck for the past five years. On the subjective intensity scale from 0 to 10 she described the pain level as being an 8. The Statement used was "I have a pain in my neck and that can change; I want that pain to go away." In order to avoid excessive repetition, from here on that kind of Statement will be called a "Standard Format Statement" (abbreviated to SFS), meaning a statement that incorporates a direct reference to the symptom. After the first round of Dynamind the intensity level went down to 2. After the second round the pain was gone.

Case P81802-Lower back pain: A woman, fifty years old, had had continuous pain in her lower back for some weeks and at the time of the session she reported the pain as being at a level 5. An SFS was used. After the first round the level came down to a 3, and after the second round the pain disappeared fully.

Case P81803-Toothache: A young woman of thirty-one had a toothache of level 5. It went down to level 3 after the first round and down to 0 after the second round.

Case P35104-Burns: The client was a man in his sixties who was experiencing residual pain from steam burns at a level 8. An SFS was used for the first round and there was slight improvement. The Statement used for the second round was, "I have learned the lesson from the burning and you can go away." The result was complete relief from the pain after the Touch and the Breath.

Case P35105-Leg cramp: A man in his sixties had been experiencing intense pain from a leg cramp at a level 10 for ten minutes. SFSs were used. After the first round the level went to 8, after the second round it went to 4, and after the third round there was no more pain.

Case P35106-Elbow pain: A woman had had pain in her right elbow for five months at a level 6. SFSs were used for three rounds and the pain level went from 5 to 3 to 0.

Case P55507-Stomach pain: The client was a twenty-nine-year-old woman with a severe pain in her stomach which she had had off and on for years. It was so bad this day that she had been to a doctor the same morning for advice. An SFS was used with the wording, "I feel a stabbing-like pain in my stomach…" After the first round the woman had an amazed look on her face because the pain had lessened to a remarkable degree and had changed from a stabbing sensation to a dull ache. An SFS was used for the second round and the pain was gone. From the case notes: "For her it was nothing less than a miracle."

Case P55508-Lower back pain: A woman of forty years had had a car accident years ago in which her back and pelvis were broken in five places. Since that time she often had enormous pain in that area which made it difficult for her to sit, and pain relievers did not help much. An SFS for a sharp pain was used for the first round and the pain went down so much that she was amazed, especially since the pain medicine she had taken shortly before hadn't worked. An SFS for a dull pain was used for the second round and the pain was completely gone. There was a follow-up the next week and the client said that each time it started to trouble her she just did the process and "the pain disappears real fast, like magic."

Case PSK09-Hand pain: A woman had level 7 pain in the top part of her left hand and could not close her fingers. An SFS for pain was used in round 1 and the pain went down to 4. After an SFS for "some pain" in the second round the pain went to 0 and she could close her hand.

Case P41910-Leg pain: The client was a forty-five-year-old woman suffering from depression who had recently been diagnosed with HIV. At the time of the session she was feeling an excruciating pain in her right leg below the knee at a level 7. SFSs were used through three rounds, going from pain, to dull pain, to numbness. Pain levels descended to a 4, then a 1, then to 0.

Case P26411-Back pain: A woman, age fifty-one, had experienced acute, toxic food poisoning from shellfish a week before the session. She had received a shot in her left hip for pain, which included an antispasmodic for intestinal distress. Since that time she had continued to feel pain in her intestines, her hip, and her lower back, and had continued to take the antispasmodic medicine. At the time of the session she was bothered by a level 4 pain in her lower back and could not bend from the waist without extreme discomfort. The first round Statement was, "I have a problem with a nagging ache across the entire small of my back…" Her pain was reduced from 4 to 1 and she could bend over and almost touch the floor. For the second round the Statement was, "I still have a problem with a nagging ache across the entire small of my back and I have proved to myself that this can be changed. I want this problem to go completely away right now." The pain was entirely gone and she could now bend over from her waist and touch the floor easily without pain.

Case P26412-Knee pain: This man, age 74, was

also a cancer client. In this session he wanted to work on the arthritis pain in both of his kneecaps, which was complicated by the presence of bone spurs. He had been experiencing this pain for six months and he described it as "mild," although he called it a level 5. He is an inventor and has an intricate knowledge of mechanics, as well as of his own body. He was fascinated by the idea of promoting healing by relieving tension. SFSs were used, adjusted as the sensation changed. The pain went to a self-described level of 3.5 in the first round, 2.5 in the second round, and a "negligible" 0.5 after the last round.

Case P15213-Headache: A woman in her forties had a headache all day which was at level 7 at the time of the session. After the first round with an SFS it went to level 2, and with the same SFS after the second round it was 0.

Case P15214-Sciatic pain: A woman in her forties had sciatica pain down her right side for 10 days. After two rounds of SFS it was nearly gone.

Case P15215-Headache: A man in his thirties had a persistent headache for three days. It took only two rounds to make it disappear. He said, "Now I can go and do a full day's work."

Case P15216-Shoulder pain: A woman in her thirties with a three-month-old pain in her right shoulder made it go away in two rounds.

Case P15217-Shoulder pain: A woman in her twenties with a level 5 pain in her shoulder for two weeks got rid of it completely in three rounds.

Case P39218-Painful bite: Here is one straight from the file. "My eight-year-old son had his finger bitten by a small dog with very sharp teeth. He came back to the house screaming and howling with pain. I gave him some Rescue Remedy, but it didn't help, so we did Dynamind. He said, 'My finger is aching and this can change. I want this pain to go away.' After the third round he just completely forgot about the matter."

Case P12419-Back pain: The client was a woman of fifty-seven with Hodgekin's Disease. Her presenting problem was pain in the trapezius muscle below the occiput, and it was noticed that her neck muscles were very stiff. She also had sounds in her right ear and a kind of twinkling in her right eye. The first round used an SFS for stress in the neck muscle, and the second round was for pain in the neck. After that the neck pain, the ear sounds, and the twinkling were all gone. An hour later she reported that all the pain in her back was gone and she could move like she was never able to do before.

Case P26420-Headache: Although this case took four rounds, I am including it here because it was still very short considering the circumstances, and it demonstrates the flexibiity of the technique, as well as the creativity of the therapist. The client was a woman, age thirty-three, who was almost completely disabled due to an automobile accident eighteen years previous to the session. She had very limited use of her right arm and legs. She could speak hesitantly from the right side of her mouth, had tremors and mild brain damage, but her intelligence did not seem to be impaired. The problem on this day was a headache that had returned periodically for the past two months and that was now at a level 3. The whole process was done in a reclining position. For the first round the Statement was, "I have a headache behind both of my eyes and this can be changed. (The therapist) will tap for me." The pain went to a level 2. A similar Statement was used for round three. The pain decreased to a 1 and became localized behind the right eye only. The Statement was modified for that and the pain went away completely.

Case P71221-Migraine: The client was a woman

with a migraine so bad it was causing her to vomit. After the first round of an SFS the migraine was gone on the left side, but it was still over her right eye. After the second round she said, "Oh my God! It's gone! Thank you!"

Emotionally-loaded Pain

Because of the layering effect of tension, the relief of surface pain often uncovers pain in other locations, as well as underlying emotional conditions that cry out for relief as well. In fact, in a large number of cases emotional relief is vital to the relief of physical symptoms. Often, in order to access this emotional resistance, assumptions of fear or anger have to be made. This is because of a strange, but pan-human, phenomenon whereby the conscious mind is unaware of the state of the body. The body of a person might be in great emotional distress, but consciously the person insists that he or she is currently not feeling any fear, anger, or other unpleasant emotion. There might be an awareness of pain or disfunction of some type, but not emotion. In my experience this happens most often with people who have developed a habit of suppressing unpleasant feelings, but it's possible for this to happen with anyone at certain times because of cultural attitudes and beliefs regarding the separation of intellect and emotions. In practice, assuming the presence of such emotions has been found to be highly effective in many cases. Following are some cases of this nature, as well as some where emotional awareness occurred as the physical pain was relieved.

Case PSK22-Stomach pain: At a dinner a woman in her fifties had a pain in her stomach and could not eat. We used an SFS for the first round without any effect. Although she was not aware of any fear she agreed to use an assumption of fear with the following Statement: "My stomach may be afraid of something…" After the second round with this Statement there was some relief, and more relief on the third round. Using the same statement there was complete relief on the fourth round.

Case P39323-Stomach pain: A man had intermittent stabbing pains around his solar plexus more or less every six months. At these times nothing provided relief and he would end up in the hospital. On this occasion, when the pain started he did two rounds with the Statement "My stomach has fear..." and the pain went away completely.

Case P12424-Back pain: A young woman of seventeen had severe pain in her back between her shoulders. Her doctor had given her strong pain pills because he could do no more for her, and he suggested that the pain might be caused by physical stress from her job as a hairdresser. She had also tried massage with no relief. Discussion with the therapist revealed fear about an upcoming test and anger with one of the women at work. For the first round the Statement was "When I think of my big test there is fear in my body..." The pressure and tension in her back eased considerably. For the second round she said, "When I think about my place of work I feel stress in my body..." The pain was completely gone. Her third round Statement was "When I think about the other woman at work I feel anger in my back muscles..." All the tension was gone and she cried with relief.

Case P12425-Elbow pain: In this case a man of fifty-eight had a level 9 pain in his left elbow and also pain in his left shoulder joint. He reported that he had had an operation on the elbow because his doctor told him there was a resistant inflammation inside and the bones had to be cleaned. A week before the session a neurologist had told the man that he could not be helped because the nerve in his elbow was injured. After the first round of an SFS for the elbow pain the intensity level dropped to 4. Since one of the things I teach is that inflammation and infection may indicate the presence of anger stressors, in addition to any other stressors directly related to a physical problem, a round for anger in the elbow was tried, and the pain level went down to a 1. A final round using an SFS for the residual pain was done and both the elbow pain and the shoulder pain were gone.

Case P81826-Headache: A man aged forty-two had had very strong attacks of headaches since his divorce three years previously, and planned to go to a hospital because of it. Initial pain at the start of the session was level 5. Using an SFS there was no change after the first round. Both fear and anger assumptions were made, but there was still no change. The therapist had an intuition that anger was involved, so the client was asked about his relationship with his father, which turned out to be a good one. Suddenly the man said that if the therapist had asked about his mother it would be a different story. After helping the man to state his feelings toward a symbolic representation of his mother, one more round of Dynamind was done with a statement referring to anger at his mother. The pain went away completely. Prior to this session the man had experienced headaches two to three times a week, but a follow-up after two months revealed that no more headaches had occurred.

Case P81827-Shoulder pain: A woman of fifty had a level 5 pain in her left shoulder for several days, making it difficult to move her arm. The first round used an SFS for sharp pain and the intensity went to 4. This therapist assumes that the left side of the body is a feminine symbol and that a sharp pain may signify anger. On questioning the client she said that she was angry at a female cousin at the time. The second round was done with the Statement "Whenever I think of my cousin I feel anger..." The pain almost disappeared then, and by the next day it was gone.

Case P35128-Ear pain: A man in his twenties had a level 8 pain in his left ear as a result of scuba diving. One round with an SFS resulted in a change in the feeling to fear in his solar plexus. One more round with an SFS for fear resulted in both pain and fear dropping to level 1. No more was done since at this level the symptoms almost always go away on their own in a relatively short time.

Case P36129-Stomach pain: A young girl of eleven had a stomach ache before going to school. After one round with an SFS the girl became aware of a feeling that her teacher was bad. For three more rounds the Statement was made that "I am afraid of my teacher and that can change; my fear is going away." At this point a new idea emerged, that the scolding was the teacher's problem, not hers. After three more rounds using that idea for the Statement the stomach ache was gone.

Case PSK30-Lower back pain: A woman in her fifties came on stage complaining of lower back pain, tingling in her legs, and pain in her left leg. The lower back pain was the strongest and was worked on first. Humming on the points was done instead of tapping. Using an SFS for the first round resulted in tingling in the lower back, but only a slight change in symptoms. For round two an assumption of anger was made with the Statement "I have a problem with my lower back being angry about something…" The back pain was less, a sensation of heat occurred, and the subject said, "The energy is flowing!" The client wanted to continue on her own.

Case P12431-Back pain: A man of thirty-six had a condition known in Europe as "Morbus Bechterew" in which the upper back becomes rounded and the shoulders close in toward the front to form a half circle. He was also in great pain. He had had the condition for twenty years and had tried Ayurveda, Feldenkrais, and other alternative therapies with little relief. After discussing his personal problems the therapist determined that the man had many fears in his life, so the Dynamind Technique began with the Statement "I have fear in my body..." and he felt more relaxed. The second round used "I have doubt in my body..." and the fear came back. Round three used the fear Statement again and he felt more relaxed. Round four used the variation "When I think about my life I have fear in my body..." and he became sure that change was really possible. Then the therapist guided him in a switch to a Power Statement, "I have the power to live without doubt..." The doubt was gone and he felt even better. In the fourth round the Power Statement was "My body has the power to be straight, yes it does, make it happen, make it so." During the Breath segment he looked different, his spine became straighter, and he lifted up his head. The fifth round Statement was "I have the power to move my body into a good posture..." After that he ran to a mirror and shouted, "Never before have I been so straight and so relaxed. Thank you!" The next day he reported that all the pain was gone.

Case P69232-Lip pain: A young man was experiencing pain in his lips at a level 7. Round one used an SFS, but there was no change. The therapist inquired as to whether anything unpleasant had happened recently and the young man stated that he was in a state of unspoken anger at his brother. The Statement for round two was "Something is burning on my lips..." and there was an immediate and significant change. A short while later his lips were normal without any other form of treatment.

Case P69233-Sore throat: A man of about fifty had a sore throat and a terrible cough for a ten days, and the cough was so strong that it gave him a headache. He said the problem was level 9-10. The session began with work on the sore throat, but there was no change after a few rounds and the therapist felt like the man did not want to let go of something. Discussion uncovered the fact that at that time the man had been reading a "spiritual" book which he enjoyed at first, began to dislike more and more as he read further. Because it was a spiritual book, though, he felt obligated to finish it. After some resistance to working on emotions, he finally agreed when he started to cough furiously. Three rounds related to anger were done and the coughing stopped and the sorness was gone.

Pain and Imagery

Practically everyone who can read a novel knows that imagination has the power to excite the emotions or stimulate the intellect. Nearly everyone who has experienced self hypnosis or guided meditation knows that imagination can induce changes in behavior. Relatively few people are aware that imagination can help to relieve pain, especially when incorporated into the Dynamind Technique. In my use of imagery, based on my shamanic training, the application is very different from simply creating a positive image. Instead, we evoke an image that represents the symptom and then we proceed to change that image in a way that results in the relief of related tension. Although an image-generating formula is available, as described in the previous chapter, most often the images come from the mind of the person doing the process though a combination of logic and intuition, plus suggestions from the therapist when necessary. The following cases will assist in expanding your awareness of that aspect of imagination's power. Remember that a "Symkey" refers to a symbolic key in the form of an image.

Case P15234-Foot pain: A man in his sixties had pain in his right foot for a month at level 5. The first round used an SFS and the pain level went down to 1. The same SFS was used for round two along with an image of a round, black one-pound knife being pulled out of his foot and thrown away, and then he was feeling fine with no pain.

Case P15235-Headache: A man in his forties had a headache in his forehead for ten months straight. At the time of the session it was level 6. There was no change after the first round using an SFS, but a second round using the same SFS brought the level of intensity to 5. The third round included an image of "a sharp grey clamp that weighs tons pressing on the sides of my head. It's now releasing and my head is free. I watch the clamp disappear into the sky. It becomes a tiny dot, and then nothing." At this point the client was feeling a bit better and the pain was just a small dot in the middle of his forehead, so he left. Ten minutes later he called to report that the pain had gone down to level 1-2. Another session was held the next day when the pain had risen again to level 5. This time it only took two rounds of SFS to bring it to 0.

Case P39236-Neck Pain: A woman in her thirties had a great deal of pain in her neck. After an SFS did not change the condition the woman said that it was the burdens she bore that made her neck so painful. The Statement was changed to "My neck is loaded with burdens…" and an image of the burdens being lifted was used. After one round of this the pain was gone.

Case P39237-Side pain: A woman of unknown age had stabbing pains in her right side. An emotional assumption was made in the form of "My right side is angry…" and an image of healing hands applying spiritual energy to the area was used. The pain in the right side was relieved and pain appeared in the lower abdomen, but shifted back to the right side. This time the assumption was made that "My kidney is in fear…" and the imaginary healing hands were applied again. The pain disappeared and did not return.

Case P39238-Shoulder pain: I like the imagery

in this one. A woman had pain in her arms when she would raise them above shoulder level. She was also receiving chiropractic treatment at the time of the session. Emotional assumption Statements were used in the form of "My arms are angry..." and "My tendons are angry..." with the addition of imagery of receiving chiropractic treatment. The pain disappeared and therapist reported that the client had not required actual chiropractic treatment for more than ten days after the session.

Case PSK39-Eye pain: A man in his late forties had strong pain around his eyes at a level 10. SFSs did not work, so Symkeys were used and expressed verbally as a Statement. The first one was "The pain around my eyes feels like there is a piece of twisted rope in there, and that can change. I am now soaking that rope in healing water until it softens and the rope comes apart." The second image described the feeling as a taut rubber band that was released and allowed to go limp. The third image was of a curved spine that was straightened and relaxed by a powerful, compassionate healer. The images came spontaneously from the client, and each time one was used the drop in pain level was dramatic. Time was given to the client to make the images as clear as possible and the whole process took ten minutes. At the end of that time the pain level was 2 and the client preferred to stop the process.

Case P26440-Migraine: A woman of forty-two had been experiencing migraine headaches for about a year, ever since the onset of early menopausal symptoms due to breast cancer surgery. Normally, her headaches started building about a week before menses. This particular headache began three days before the session and culminated at a high level 5 when her eyes were open and she "sees the light." Round one used an SFS for a specific description of the headache and the intensity lowered to 3.5. The intensity rose to 4 during the second round Statement and dropped back to 3.5 after the Breath. For the third round the following imagery was used: "My headache feels like I am wringing out water from a twisted rag. The water is dripping out until no more water falls. As I shake out the towel and hang it up to dry I see my headache leaving." The client reported that she felt better and could now keep her eyes open with a "solid, bearable, level 3 headache." She later reported that she had continued the process, including the imagery, before falling asleep and that she awoke three hours later with no headache.

Case P13141-Foot pain: An administrative nurse of fifty who studies healing on the side came to a session with pain in her right foot from an accident which involved a fracture from a fall. She had previously had surgery on both feet some years before. The pain level was 5-6 and was only felt when she walked. This client had some difficulty in making the motivation segment of the Statement, preferring to say, "I'd like the pain to go away," rather than "I want the pain to go away." After some rounds using SFS with very little change the therapist asked if there were any images and the client said, "I see little demons coming out of my foot." This imagery was used in the next round, but the change only resulted in a level 4 for the pain. Then the therapist suggested that the client include imagery from the previous surgery. After a number of rounds using different images that came to the client there was no significant change until the client said, "I'm realizing that my medical background and experience of it taking a long time to heal are getting in the way here." The therapist suggested that the client apply the Huna principle of "There are no limits" (the client was unfamiliar with Huna before this). The client agreed, and for the next Statement she said, "I need to change this belief I have had about healing and time, because I realize there really is no time limit, and I want to to change my belief system from time to no limits." The client was asked to walk and the pain had changed to level 3. Several more rounds using suggested imagery did not produce any further change until the therapist asked the client to simply notice any images that came up when she made her Statements. After round 10 the client said "There's a circle form near real tall buildings. It's awesome, overpowering, a little scary. I imagine myself down in that. So I could change it by seeing myself on top, looking down. So should I imagine that?" The therapist wisely said, "Sure!" And the level went down to 2, the first significant change in quite a while. At this point the session ended because it had been two hours. Some days later the therapist met the client at a meeting and asked her about the pain in her foot. The client said, "What foot? What pain?"

Case P35142-Headache: A middle-aged woman had a headache at level 7. After using the same SFS for three rounds the pain level only reduced to level 5. For the next round the same statement was used, accompanied by a symbol of a raging ocean being changed into a shallow lagoon. This resulted in a sensory shift to a feeling of fear in her right eyebrow, temple, and jaw. An SFS applied to the temple resulted in a reduction of the fear where it had been and the appearance of the fear feeling in her brow. Emotional assumptions for unhappiness and doubt were made and resulted in a 4.5 level of tension in the forehead. Then came a feeling of not having grieved enough about something in her life. When this was used as a Statement it brought tears and a feeling of tension in the crown of her head. This SFS was used again and brought the tension down to a 4. The symbol of a wilted flower growing and being nourished with fertilizer and rain brought more tears and a feeling of tension in the right temple, plus an awareness of missing her mother and a feeling of anger that brought the tension in the crown back up to 4.5. Use of an SFS brought the tension down to a level of 3.5 in the right eye, and one more for that location brought it down to a 3. At this point the client felt relieved enough to end the session.

Case P35143-Sunburn: A middle-aged man had a severe sunburn with a pain intensity level of 8. After three rounds of SFSs the level went down to 5. Then the same statement was used along with an image of being on fire and jumping into a pool of ice cubes. The pain level immediately became a 1 and the redness turned into a tan by the end of the next day with no peeling.

Case P55544-Knee pain: A man about thirty years old had hurt his left knee severely on the tennis court. He had a large scrape wound and his knee swelled up enormously. Bending his knee was extremely painful and made it difficult drive his car, which he needed to do for his business. An SFS for a nasty pain in his left knee did not result in any change. A Standard Image was used for the next Statement as follows: "I have a pain in my left knee which is like a black ball weighing two kilograms, and this can change. I want this ball to go away." Then an angel was asked to come and take the ball away, but in the client's mind the angel said it was too heavy to lift. The therapist suggested that he ask the angel if a crane would help. In the man's imagery another angel came with a crane and the two angels put the chains around the ball and used the crane to lift it out of his knee, and then they flew away with the ball. Tapping and breathing followed this, to no avail. The exact same Statement and imagery was used two more times with no apparent change. A follow-up report revealed that the swelling was completely gone by the next day and the man played tennis with his friends, who had expected him to be unable to play for weeks. At the end of one week his knee was healing nicely on the outside without any scars. This shows that not all changes take place during the session itself.

Case PSK45-Arm pain: A woman in her forties had pain in both arms. Round one used an SFS for the pain with no change. Round two used "My left arm is angry..." with a small change. For the third round a Symkey in the form of a thick pin in her arm was used to represent the pain and mentally removed three times. At the end of that round the arm was fine and pain appeared in her left hand. The same Symkey was used in the fourth round and the pain in her hand was gone.

Case P69246-Foot pain: The imagery used in a Dynamind session does not always have to be in the form of a symbol that represents the symptom. Here is a case where memory was used in a creative way. The client was a teacher who had had pain in one of the toes of her right foot for three weeks. She was concerned that it might have been broken and she planned to consult a doctor after the session. An SFS for the pain in her toe did not bring any relief, and she expressed skepticism as to whether this technique could help her. The therapist asked her when the pain had started. At first she could not remember, but eventually she recalled being in a pool while giving a swimming lesson. She had stepped in a small hole at the bottom of the pool with her toe and had twisted it. For the next round, only the second in the session, the same SFS was repeated with the addition of the memory of being in the pool without stepping into the hole. This was only done once, as the client wanted to leave. Some days later she reported that she had not gone to the doctor because the pain had gone and her toe was fine.

Case P55547-Back pain: The client, a woman of twenty-eight, reported that she had a pain in her upper back for the past two or three years, which she attributed to working at a computer. Round one of Dynamind with an SFS did not produce significant change. When the therapist said that she didn't have any such problem working at a computer the client replied that maybe it would be a good idea to change her own ideas about that kind of work. The client added that her colleagues didn't have such a problem either. Imagery was added to the next round. "I have a little pain in my back which feels like a small, purple/green line weighing about three grams. This can change. I want this pain to go away." An angel came and took the line and flew off with it. After the tapping and the breathing the pain was gone.

Fibromyalgia

According to the National Institute of Arthritis and Musculoskeletal and Skin Diseases, this condition, sometimes called fibrositis, is a chronic disorder that causes pain and stiffness throughout the tissues that support and move the bones and joints. Pain and localized tender points occur in the muscles, particularly those that support the neck, spine, shoulders, and hips. The disorder includes widespread pain, fatigue, and sleep disturbances. It is difficult to diagnose because the symptoms mimic so many other conditions. Treatment centers around management, not cure, and generally includes a combination of exercise, physical therapy, and medication. All of the following cases involve clients with medically diagnosed fibromyalgia.

Case PSK48: The client was a woman in her late forties with chronic facial pain. We used a combination of SFSs and imagery to clear many layers of tension pain on the right side of her face, her jaw, and her forehead. Imagery included symbols to relieve pressure, the dissolving of an egg, the use of spirit helpers in the removal of a whole sea of black stuff, and the use of an angelic welder to remove a metal plate dividing her brain. After forty-five minutes she was free of pain and she said, "It feels funny not to have the pain any more."

Case P41949: The client was a woman in her fifties with fibromyalgia. She complained about a pain in her thumbs which she blamed on damp weather. The first Statement was "When I bend my thumbs there is a shooting pain and that can change..." There was a lessening of the pain, so the second round used the same statement and then the pain was gone.

Case P26450: The client was a woman who had suffered from fibromyalgia for the past five years, and had migrating pain in twelve of the eighteen Fibromyalgia "hotspots." The session was conducted by telephone and the woman was first given instructions about how to do the Dynamind Technique. At the time of the session she was experiencing a 6.5 level of discomfort. The first Statement was "I feel a numbness and burning from my right knee to my right ankle. I know this feeling can be changed. I want this feeling of numbness and burning to go away." This reduced the discomfort level to 4. The second round Statement was modified to include the words "I have proved to myself that this can be changed..." After this the sensations were reduced to "just a tiny bit of numbness." The sensation remained at this level over the next twenty minutes of general discussion.

Case P26451: A woman aged forty-eight, recently diagnosed with fibromyalgia. Work on this condition began after six rounds of Dynamind involving the reduction of knee and foot pain from an automobile accident from 4 to 1 and 4 to 2, respectively. The woman chose to work on what she considered to be one of the most annoying manifestations, that of a sharp pain above and below her left elbow which had persisted for the last four months and which made it painful to lift anything. Since she had already lifted a book and a glass during the session she was asked to rate these on the intensity scale. She gave the book-lifting an 8 and the glass-lifting a 6. After two rounds using direct SFSs the respective pains were reduced to 4 and 3. Although she chose to end the session there, it is worth noting that she achieved a 50% reduction of pain in a one-minute application of the Dynamind Technique.

Additional Anecdotes

Case PX52-Leg Pain: "During a conference my legs, and especially my knees, had been aching and very uncomfortable. By the third day of the conference the pain had risen to a distraction level, so I decided to do something about it and did Dynamind while sitting in the hotel lobby. I did about six or seven rounds and then just leaned back to relax. Within seconds I forgot all about my legs and the next time I thought about them the pain was 95% gone."

Case PX53-Migraine: "After attending Serge's Dynamind workshop I went to a breakfast meeting where a colleague complained of a migraine headache. I took her to sit by the river and asked her to tell me the intensity on a scale of 0-10. She said 200!. I guided her through the Dynamind process and within fifteen minutes the pain level was down to 4. Not bad for the first time!"

Case PX54-Leg pain: "I tried out the Dynamind technique on myself first and it worked great. I pulled something on the back of my leg. It was pressing on a nerve and I was getting this jolting pain. I used your technique and after twice it was completely gone. What a relief that was. On a scale of 1-10 it was an 8. The next time I tried it was on this heavy energy located at the front of my head. The same results. I have also helped some of my friends get rid of migraines and an inner ear pain. My friends appear at my desk at work when they need help."

Case PX55-Smoke pain: "I wanted to let you

know about a personal healing that I did using the Dynamind technique. I had inhaled some smoke that burned my throat and into my lungs causing a burning and coughing sensation. When I did the process and got to the point to tell the pain to go away, I felt a strong urge instead to tell it to "heal" so I said this aloud before each tapping and it was amazing. First, I felt myself go deep into the pain sensation and then it started to dissipate from the inside out. It took only one more time for it to go away about 95%. It was a really good experience and also taught me to discover what words and images may work best for each situation."

Chapter Four
RELIEVING OTHER AILMENTS

The Dynamind Technique has proven effective in helping to relieve the symptoms of a large number of physical ailments in addition to the relief of pain. This chapter will present cases related to this kind of application. The cases described for a particular type of ailment may include direct symptom relief, emotional shifting or emotional assumptions, and the use of imagery. This, of course, is merely a sampling of the many different conditions for which the Dynamind Technique has been used. And, while the emphasis here is on succesful outcomes, it must be kept in mind that Dynamind is not always effective for everyone, and it is only recommended in cases where the relief of tension can contribute to improvement in a given condition.

Tinnitus

Tinnitus, properly pronounced in English as either TINnitus or TinNIGHTus, is a medical term for the perception of sound in one or both ears, or in the head, when there is no external sound present. Although it is often referred to as a "ringing in the ears," it may just as well take the form of roaring, hissing, chirping, whistling, or clicking. It might be occasional or constant with one or more tones present, and the perceived volume may range from soft to extremely loud.

According to the American Tinnitus Association the

physiological cause or causes are unknown, except that there seems to be an obvious relationship to being exposed to loud noises. Other recognized factors are wax build-up in the ear canal, side-effects from certain kinds of medications, ear or sinus infections, jaw misalignment, cardiovascular disease, some types of tumors, and head or neck trauma.

There is no acknowledged cure, but some people have experienced relief by such varied means as nutritional or herbal supplements, acupuncture, magnets, hypnosis, biofeedback, electrode implants, behavioral change, drug therapy, TMJ (temporomandibular joint) treatment, and Tinnitus Retraining Therapy (which can take 12 to 24 months).

As I indicated in my book, *Instant Healing*, when many different methods of treatment accomplish the same thing, the likelihood is that they are all doing one thing. Obviously, the one thing I think they are all doing is relieving tension.

My first attempt to guide someone in using Dynamind for tinnitus was not very successful, in spite of including emotional assumptions and imagery. This led me to wonder where the tension was. Then one day as I was sitting at my desk I stretched my head back against my spine and I suddenly experienced the symptoms of tinnitus. When I brought my head back up it was gone. Since then I have found that this happens to virtually everyone. When I considered the cause it seemed clear that my head action was stressing the muscles in the back of my neck and along my shoulders. So I thought that perhaps a high enough level of shoulder tension might bring on the effects of tinnitus, at least in some people. What happens in fact is that, overall, we get much better results in relieving tinnitus when the shoulder and neck muscles are relaxed first. This will not be apparent in some of the cases below, but I believe it is a critical factor.

Case OSK01: A middle-aged woman with tinnitus. Two rounds of Dynamind with SFSs had no result. I asked if there were any sensations in her body when she thought about the tinnitus and she said that she felt stiffness and pain along her left neck and shoulder. We relieved both of those symptoms with SFSs and her face lit up with pleasure and surprise as the tension eased. We went back to the tinnitus and I asked her what the sound reminded her of. She said it was like a jet engine, so I suggested that she throttle it down. She tried and said she couldn't because "the wires were broken." Then I suggested that she call in an angel mechanic and with that she got some relief. She chose to continue on her own.

Case OSK02: A woman in her forties with tinnitus. First, with SFSs modifed as symptoms changed, we cleared many layers related to exhaustion, anger, perfectionism, and tension in the shoulders and neck. Then we worked directly on the tinnitus and achieved a considerable amount of relief before the session ended.

Case OSK03: A man in his thirties with tinnitus in his right ear at a level 4. For the first round we used an SFS with a Symkey of a high-frequency saw and a dial being turned down, which reduced it to a level 3.5. Rounds two and three used SFSs for shoulder tension, which took nearly all of that away. Round four was for tension in the right ear, and the sound went down to a level 1.

Case OSKS04: A man in his forties who had had tinnitus for years. Round one was used to relieve shoulder tension. Round two was for tension in the ear with a Symkey of a sound machine with a dial to turn the sound down. After this the sound was gone and a pain appeared at the 7th cervical vertebra. Round three used an SFS for the pain and the pain and tinnitus were gone.

Case O39205: A man had had ringing in the ears

for twenty years due to a bomb explosion in a war. The noise was sometimes deafening and the doctors said he had a hole in his eardrum, making it an irreversible condition. The therapist used a combination of "My ears have fear" and "My ears have stress," plus the imagery of a radio dial to bring the volume down. It took fifteen rounds to bring the intensity down from a level 10 to a level 2, an 80% reduction of the problem in less than half an hour. Some time after the client reported that when he was under great stress the sound rose in volume again, but that he was able to lower it again to a "slight background noise" using the Dynamind Technique.

Case O12406: This session took place during dinner in a restaurant with a woman of forty-seven who had had tinnitus in her left ear "for a long time." The noise was like water rushing through a pipe at level 8. Round one used an SFS with tension around the ear, and this lowered the sound level to 4. Round two used a statement that there was a pipe noise in her left ear, plus a radio dial image used during the Breath segment. No change. Round three used a noise statement and the radio dial imagined vividly before the Touch segment and the level went to 0. That was a 100% change in three minutes.

Case O12407: A woman of forty-five with tinnitus in both ears at level 7 for about eight years. Extensive clearing of physical and emotional tension was done before working on the tinnitus. Round one focused on the noise itself with no change. For round two the same SFS was used with an image added. The therapist suggested a radio dial, but the client said the sound was more like a water fall and she could imagine diverting the water so that it ran a different way. This was done and the sound was reduced to a level 3. Then for round three the following Statement was used: "There is still a noise like a waterfall and a big tension and pressure in both of my ears, but that can change. I don't want to hear this noise and I do not like the tension any longer." At the end of this round the level was 0. This demonstrates that an important factor in the application of Dynamind is to use both imagery and wording that is derived from or suitable to the person doing it.

Respiratory Problems

This section includes problems related to shortness of breath, asthma attacks, sinus problems, nose blockage, and other respiratory ailments in which pain, if it is present, is a secondary consideration.

Case OSK08-Shortness of breath: A woman in her thirties came on stage for a demonstration with a four-year-old problem of difficulty in breathing after exertion. She agree to run a short distance of about forty feet (twelve meters) and reported difficulty breathing. Round one used that phrase in the SFS and she felt a lot better. She ran again twice the aforementioned distance and report that she still had some difficulty. That phrase was incorporated into the next round. Then she felt so good she ran about three times the first distance and and then she reported that she had no problem at all.

Case OSK09-Clogged sinuses: A man in his forties came on stage with clogged sinuses at a level 5. The first round used an SFS for clogged sinuses with a small change. Round two used the phrase "My sinuses are frustrated..." and the condition went to a level 2, but a new layer with a symptom of burning in the chest became evident. The third round was for the burning in the chest and there was complete relief.

Case OSK10-No smelling: This is not exactly a respiratory problem, but it is a nose problem, so I am including it here. A woman in her thirties had no sense of smell for the previous six months. We only had time for one round for "smelling properly," but aside from some clearing of tension around her nose there was no other result. However, the next day she reported that her sense of smell was coming back. This is a good example of a delayed effect that frequently happens with the Dynamind Technique.

Case O39211-Blocked nose: A woman had a completely blocked nose and she felt weak and shivery, as if she were coming down with a cold. An SFS for "My nose is blocked…" caused her nose to open a bit, and after a second round of the same she could breath easily. On the next round "I am feeling bad…" was tried for the rundown feeling, but it didn't help. The client mentioned having worked all day with her boss, so an emotional assumption of anger at her boss was used for the third round and she felt much better.

Case O12412-Blocked nose: A woman of twenty reported that her nose was always blocked and she could not breathe very well. As this client was already known to the therapist an anger assumption was suggested and the client agreed to try it. The first round with a general Statement about anger in the body brought some relief, and a second round using anger in the nose relieved the condition.

Case O12413-Blocked nose et al.: A young girl of fifteen was preparing to move from one parent's home to the other's a few years after the parents had divorced. During this time she experienced nose blockage, neck and chest pains, headache and tiredness with an overall perceived intensity level of 9. The symptoms were those of an allergy or a cold, but also of suppressed anger, so the session began with an anger assumption in the form of "There is anger in my body…" The intensity dropped to level 8. The next round used a decision Statement that I have named "Blanket Forgiveness" and which had not been used before as part of the Dynamind Technique. "Whatever this is related to, I forgive it completely, and it doesn't matter any more." After making this Statement, plus the tapping and breathing, the intensity fell to a level 2, but the nose was still closed. On the third round the client used "There is still some anger in my nose…" and the level went to 0. Later observation showed even more changes. Until the time of the session the girl's hands were deep red, diagnosed by a doctor as neurodermatitis, and after the session they returned to a normal color. Also, she no longer had stomach cramps during menses.

Case O25814-Sinus infection: The client, a woman, apparently had a sinus infection with an ache at level 8. The first round used the SFS "I have an ache in my cheek…" and the symptom changed to a pulsing in the cheek at level 2. A second round SFS resulted in another change of symptom and location to a pressure in the ear, still at level 2. Further rounds uncovered tension layers with pulsing in a tooth, slow pulsing in the sinus, and pressure in the eyes. At this point the therapist suggested an anger assumption. This led to sadness on the whole right side of the client's head. A round for sadness led to crying and a relief of all symptoms. The client said, "I had no idea there was such an emotional component to my sinus problem."

Case O69215-Various respiratory symptoms: A young woman had felt feverish for a week, with a sore throat, congestion in her chest, and a closed nose. Standard rounds relieved the throat and chest symptoms, but the nose condition was resistant to change. Finally the Statement "There is something out there that my nose is full of…" was used. The client reported hearing a "ping" sound and her nose and head were completely open. She was very astonished and happy.

Case 069216-Coughing attack: The therapist was with a friend in a movie theater when the friend suddenly had a terrible coughing fit. The friend was about to leave in order not to disturb the other patrons, so the therapist took a minute to explain the Dynamind Technique. The client used the SFS "There is an itching in my throat…" and "There is an awful itching in my throat…" and he immediately calmed down. During the evening the therapist noticed that his friend did the tapping a few times and later the friend said that he was saying the words mentally. As the therapist reported, "We had a very quiet time, with almost no coughing at all."

Case O69217-Another closed nose: A male client complained that his left nostril had been closed for two days. He gave it a level 9 intensity. For about fifteen minutes various Statement with the process resulted in no significant or lasting relief. Finally the therapist reviewed mentally what he had learned about Dynamind and suggested the words, "I have a problem with a woman…" which the client tried. The nose opened fully within two minutes and stayed open. (SK comment: This was based on information from my book, *Imagineering for Health*, in which I talk about problems on the left side of the body often being associated with problems with female relationships or feminine qualities).

Case O35118-Shortness of breath: The client was a middle-aged man whose problem was shortness of breath with an intensity level of 6. The first round used the SFS "I have a feeling of congestion…" He felt slightly better, but a pain appeared in the left rear side of his lungs. For the second round an SFS was used for the pain and the the breathing problem was reduced to a 0 level.

Case O41919-Asthma attack: The client was a man in his forties, a heroin user currently on a low dose of methodone. He came to a session, but wanted to leave right away because he was in the middle of an asthma attack. The first round was done for "difficulty breathing" and there was some relief, but he wanted to go home and use his asthma machine. The therapist suggested that there might be some fear involved and would he be willing to stay and work on that. The client agreed, and the next round was for "I have a problem with fear..." This brought the level of discomfort down to only 10% of what it had been by the client's reckoning. At this point he noticed that his back was tense, so the third round was done for that symptom. Afterward he felt much more relaxed, said that he was able to notice pictures on the wall that he hadn't seen when he came in, and he had no difficulty breathing.

Case OX20: "Yesterday in the evening my boyfriend had what seemed to be an allergy reaction in his eyes and nose, so I guided him through Dynamind for anger and it went away very quickly. He said that it felt as if a stone had passed from his stomach through his feet and into the ground."

Intestinal Problems

There are many kinds of intestinal problems, all of which are considered by the medical establishment to have specific, physical causes, either bacterial, viral or functional. Medicine and surgery remain the primary methods of choice for their relief. Without denying the effect of physical stressors, there are times when relieving the tension caused by emotional stressors will lead to a resolution of the problem. This section will include intestinal problems in which any pain that might be present is secondary to the condition.

Case OSK21-Pain sensation: This demonstration case began with a complaint of pain, but quickly moved on to other issues. It concerned a woman who had had a sensation of pain at the end of her intestine for five years at a level of 4.5, which also caused her difficulty in sitting. Round one was for pain, but there was very little change.

The Statement for round two was "There is fear at the end..." and a small change occurred. The next round used "The end of my intenstine is holding onto something..." and this brought the intensity to a 3. Round four used "The end of my intestine is resisting something..." and this made the pain more diffused. For round five she said "I feel a sense of contracting at the end of my intestine..." and this had a better effect. Because of the time factor I suggested that she continue on her own, and at the end of the day she reported that all the pain and discomfort were gone.

Case O12422-Stomach pain: The client was a woman of twenty-nine, mother of three children, and in the tenth week of pregnancy. During discussion she said that she felt guilty because of problems with the children, and pressured with money problems because her husband was still in training for his profession. She also stated her need to be perfect. The stomach pain was given as level 9. Round one dealt with doubts in her body, and the level went to 6. Round two dealt with fear and it dropped further to 4. Round three was for anger in her body and the level dropped even further to 1. The Statement for the last round was "When I think of my husband there is anger and pain in my stomach..." The symptom was gone and she felt a kind of lightness within herself.

Case O81823-Nausea: A middle-aged woman felt sick to her stomach after a short meditation. During the meditation she had been thinking of a recent decision about which she had some doubts. At the time of the session she felt like vomiting and her face was grey. For the first round the Statement used was "Whenever I think about the decision I'm afraid of having made the wrong decision, and that can change. I want this fear to go away." She felt a little better and her color improved. The therapist had the woman hold an onyx stone and a minute or two later the physical and emotional symptoms were gone.

Case O81824-Diverticulitis: A man of fifty-five had suffered from intestinal inflammation for a period of some months. He stated that he worked very hard as a corporate trainer and did not like to delegate authority to others. Pain level was 6-7. There was only time for one round because the man was leaving on a trip, so an SFS was used for the inflammation. This lowered the level to 3. The client was provided with written instructions on how to do the Dynamind Technique by himself. Three weeks later the client reported that the inflammation was gone, thanks to Dynamind. He also said that he was thinking of delegating more to others to reduce his work load.

Case O26425-Intestinal gas: This case is a good example of how tension layers operate. It involves a woman sixty-five years of age who had complained for thirty years of intestinal trouble that restricted her from journeying very far from lavatory facilities for any appreciable length of time. Her "standard" discomfort level was described as 6. For round one the Statement was "I feel an irritable, gaseous pressure in my entire intestinal tract from my waist downward. This can be changed. I want this feeling to go away." There was no change in the feeling of pressure and she reported that she had difficulty getting her breath to move much further than her midriff (recall that the focus of the Breath segment is from the top of the head to the feet). For the second round a very similar Statement was used and the therapist suggested that the client "blow" the breath downward. This time there was a shift to a new tension level with a focus of pain and nausea of level 3 at the top of her stomach, in the center of the bottom of her rib cage. The third round used an appropriate SFS with an emphasis on the Breath. The nausea went away, but the pain remained and a new symptom of "gurgling" appeared. After round four the pain went away and there was a level three gas pressure in her back by her waist and kidney area. After the next round the pressure was gone and the client reported feeling that the gas was rising up the front of her body as if it wanted to escape. At this point she burped, which she was rarely able to do, and began yawning a great deal (yawning is a common response to tension release). The result of the sixth round, which dealt with the feelings in her esophagus, was a level 2 pressure in the center of her chest. After the seventh round the pressure became "a shadow of itself, less than a level 1."

Case O35126-Upset Stomach: The client was a child who had an upset stomach for about fifteen minutes at level 7. The round one Statement was "I have a yukky feeling in my stomach..." There was no change. The same Statement was used for round two and the intensity went to level 5. Round three used "I still have some feeling of upset in my stomach..." The level went to 4. Round four used the same Statement and an image was added. The child imagined the stomach discomfort as a cup of mud, and changed it to a cup of pink, fluffy, marshmallow stuff. The level moved to 2 and the session ended. A short time later the child was seen eating a sweet snack.

Case O55527-Bloating: A woman client complained that she could not eat most foods because they caused her stomach to bloat and make her look pregnant. Her doctors could find no reason for this problem. At the time of the session she had eaten something on her "forbidden" list and she was experiencing the bloating problem. The Statement used for the first round was "I have an uncomfortable feeling in my stomach..." Her stomach became very hot, so the second round Statement was "I have an uncomfortable hot feeling in my stomach..." There was no change. Anger and fear assumptions were tried without result. Finally, the therapist used the standard image formula which produced the Statement "I have an uncomfortable, hot, red and black, two-kilo feeling in my stomach which resembles my body shape…" In addition, the client visualized a spirit helper who removed that object out of her stomach and took it away. At the end of that round the client said that her stomach was cold and her jeans were not tight any longer. She was amazed.

Case O55528-Acid Reflux: Also called "heartburn" in the United States, this is a condition in which stomach acid rises up into the esophagus and a burning sensation is felt in the chest or in the lower part of the throat. Normally, there is a muscle at the bottom of the esophagus, or gullet, which keeps the acid from rising, but it is not known why the muscle sometimes does not operate correctly. What is known is that this condition is often directly related to pregnancy, smoking, eating large meals (especially near bedtime), being overweight, bending over a lot, or wearing tight clothing around the waist. Antacid medicine is the most common way to treat the problem, but surgery may be used as well in extreme cases.

In this session the client was a woman of fifty-five who experienced acid reflux often enough to receive special medicine from her doctor. At the time of the session she was feeling the pain of acid reflux, but did not have her medicine available. An SFS was used for the pain in the first round and the pain lessened. Several more rounds kept reducing the pain until the problem was gone (no pain and no acid). That night she experienced the problem again, but instead of getting up to reach for her medicine, which was her normal behavior, she used Dynamind with the Statement "I have a problem with stomach acid coming up…" The problem was resolved with one round and she went back to sleep. Some weeks later she reported that she was continuing to use Dynamind instead of the medicine and it was working perfectly. It may be that stress tension is interfering with the gullet muscle's ability to keep the stomach acid down, and that when Dynamind relieves the tension the muscle is able to function properly.

Allergies and Skin Problems

While most theories about allergies and skin problems focus on reactions to substances, I have always had excellent results for myself and others by releasing physical and emotional tension.

Case 15229-Cold sore: The medical term for this condition when it occurs on the face is Herpes Simplex Type 1. The cause is supposed to be a type of virus infection which results in small, fluid-filled blisters on the skin that ooze liquid and form a crust when they break. After appearing they generally last from seven to ten days. The only recognized medical treatment takes the form of oral anti-viral medicine. Otherwise a person with this condition is just expected to let it run its course. Personally, I have tried a folk remedy consisting of dabbing the sore with skim milk, and it seemed to me that it speeded up the healing. However, I have achieved the best results by using Dynamind at the first indication.

The case at hand involved a man in his fifties who had had a cold sore on his lower lip for two and a half weeks. In the session the first two rounds with an SFS did not result in any change, but the third round included an image of shrinking and there was some improvement. Over the next few hours it actually dried up and looked smaller, but it had opened up by the next day. The client continued to use Dynamind on his own and the day after that it had dried up again and appeared half the size. Five days after the session it was gone (SK comment: It would have been interesting to try anger assumptions on this one).

Case O25830-Itching: A woman client was having an allergic, itching reaction on both of her arms at level 5. The first round SFS included both arms and sensations went to level 3. The second round focused on the itching in the right arm and the level went to 2, but the sensation became one of "rawness." Using that word in the Statement for the third round resulted in both arms becoming free from all discomfort.

Case O69231-Eczema: A middle-aged man had eczema on his right wrist which was itching badly at a level of 9.5. He had already scratched his skin to open wounds. The first round Statement used the word "eczema" and there was no change. The second round Statement used the word "itching" and there was a decrease in the itching sensation. After a few more rounds in this manner he felt total relief, and the wounds even looked better. After one day with no further treatment of any kind the scars were almost gone. It is worth noting here that "eczema" is an abstract label and "itching" describes a sensation. We consistently get better results in almost every case when we use descriptive rather than abstract words except, curiously, when we use the word "problem." I suspect it is because the word "problem" evokes something very specific in the client's mind, whereas a word like "eczema" would be more suitable for a dermatologist.

Case O69232-Pimple: This is only one of many similar cases. The client was a young woman with a large pimple on her face that had been bothering her for quite a while. An SFS was used (the case report does not say for how many rounds) and the next day the pimple had vanished.

Case O12433-Allergies: A young man of eighteen working as a carpenter had coughing problems and was diagnosed by a doctor as being allergic to the building materials. Some discussion with the therapist revealed that he had angry feelings toward his boss and toward his father. Round one of Dynamind dealt with anger in his body, and round two dealt with anger in his lungs. The coughing stopped. Round three used the Statement "Whatever my boss and my father did or did not do with me, I forgive them completely and it doesn't matter any more." After the Dynamind session he had a two-hour session of Hawaiian massage. A few days later he reported that a blood test given by the doctor to determine which materials he was allergic to produced only negative results. He was also able to gain weight and perform his job with less stress.

Case O71234-Skin rash: The client was a boy of eleven with a rash over his whole body. After the first round with an SFS the boy was asked if he felt any change. His answer was "Not really," but the therapist observed some emotional response. After round two and the same question his response was "Maybe a little" and his emotional state was more visible. The therapist asked whether the boy was feeling sad or angry and he said, "No, I don't think so." At the same time his whole face became red and tears started. A round was tried with the Statement "My body is holding my emotions as a rash." His response to the change question was "I don't know" and the tears became less. Another round with the same Statement ended the tears and the rash looked better, but the boy did not want to continue. Ordinarily this would seem like an unsatisfactory conclusion. However, in a later report by the mother of the boy she said that she and her son were at home when she discovered that she had lost her bank deposit bag. She became so stressed that she got a visual migraine and was seeing black spots. Her son told her to stop and do Dynamind because there was an emotional connection. They did it together and the headache was gone by the time they walked across the room to leave.

Eye Problems

I have a good friend who is an eye surgeon and although he is an excellent student of the mind-body connection, we still have friendly disagreements on just how much influence physical and emotional tension relief can have on healing the eyes. So I dedicate the presentation of these cases to him.

Case O12435-Nearsightedness: The client was a man of thirty-seven whose need for glasses began with an automobile accident ten years previous in which his shoulders were broken and there was trauma to his brain and lungs. After a general release of tension the session started with the fear assumption "I have fear in my eyes..." More rounds using fear assumptions were done, then SFSs for tension in the eyes and the inability to see far. The session ended with the Power Statement "My body has the power to see things in the distance clear and well..." After this he was able to drive his car without glasses. He reported later that if he was stressed by fear and anger he needed the glasses again, so the therapist told him to use Dynamind whenever he experienced fear or anger. At last report the man did not need his glasses any more and, as a side effect of the work with fear and anger, he was able to move his arms over his head, which he could not do before.

Case O69236-Weak eyes: A middle-aged woman had observed for several months that her right eyesight was getting worse, especially in stressful situations at work and elsewhere. Before she came for a session she had been using special glasses without much success. She gave the problem a level of 8. She started out with a Statement that "There is tension in my right eye," but she had better results with a different idea that came out of that: "My right eye has a weakness that my father also had, and that can change. I want all karmic influence to dissolve." She continued to use that Statement with Dynamind for the next two weeks on her own and reported that she almost never had to use her glasses any more. She was determined to continue until her eyes were completely healed.

Case OSK37-Nearsightedness: A woman in her thirties who was nearsighted came on stage and without her glasses she could see only colors and hair when she looked at the people in the first row. I had her close her eyes during the Dynamind Technique and open them after the Breath in order to notice any improvement more easily. The first round was for tension in the eyes and then she could see spaces where the eyes would be on the faces of the people. Round two was again for tension and she could see the people even better. For round three I incorporated an image exercise that I often use for people with suspected eye tension problems. I have the person imagine that their eyes are really at the end of two tunnels that go all the way to the back of the head. I also remind them that they don't have to try and reach out with their eyes to see anything because the light is coming to them all by itself. Then I ask them to let the light come through the tunnels to their eyes at the back of the head. At the end of this round the woman could see the people much more clearly. I believe that a major factor in some vision problems is the presence of poor viewing habits.

Case OSK38-Nearsightedness: A woman in her forties with a problem of nearsightedness could only see the print on a piece of paper when it was about four inches (10 cm) from her face. The SFS in round one was "I cannot see clearly in my right eye…" and after she could see the print about twice as well at eight to ten inches (about 20-25cm). Based on a comment she made we used an emotional assumption with "My right eye is feeling guilty about something…" and she was able to see the print at twenty inches (50 cm). Another major factor in vision problems for some people is emotional tension related to something they subconsciously do not want to see. The next case illustrates this even more clearly.

Case OSK39-Fearsightedness: A woman in her forties onstage was unable to see people in the front row clearly without her glasses. Round one for tension in her eyes. She could see people on the left side of the front row a little better, but not the people directly in front. For round two we made an emotional assumption that her eyes were afraid of something and her vision actually worsened. For round three we used the Statement "Whatever my eyes are afraid of is not important any more, and I want to be able to open my eyes without fear." She began to cry and there was a feeling of sadness in the upper part of her body. Round four was done for the sadness. She felt much better and she could see all the people in the front row much better.

Case O69640-Jagged lines: A woman of thirty-eight was frequently experiencing deviation of the eyeballs and zig-zag figures in front of her eyes. There are a number of medical terms for deviation of the eyeballs, depending on the nature of the deviation. The medical term for the perception of jagged lines in one's vision is "ophthalmic migraine," meaning a migraine without a headache. It is supposed to be caused by a spasm of blood vessels in the brain, which doctors define as a migraine. For the client in question this condition would last up to two hours. During a telephone session in which she was experiencing the problem she described it to the therapist as being at a level 8. In the first round she said "I am seeing zig-zag figures and that can change; I want the zig-zag figures to disappear." The effect of this was a report of seeing fewer figures and the intensity of the experience had lowered to 5. Since she had mentioned having problems with her husband and children before the session this subject was used for the second round with the

Statement "When I think about my husband and children I feel overwhelmed..." After this she reported feeling much better, and the intensity of the eye problem had reduced to 3. Another round with the same Statement resulted in her stating that she was breathing deeply and cheerfully, she was seeing normally, feeling relaxed, and the level of the problem was 0 after only a few minutes.

Cancer

No medical cure has been found for this disease in spite of huge amounts of money dedicated to many years of research. Conventional treatment still consists of chemotherapy, radiation treatments, and/or surgery, although many alternative therapies have also been put forward, and there are a number of cases reported in which cancerous tumors have completely disappeared as a result of drastic changes in lifestyle, consistent prayer, positive expectation, and for reasons simply unknown. Unfortunately, these latter examples are not so easily replicated. It is well established, though, at least in some medical circles, that fear and anger play a very important role in the formation and spread of cancer, but the extent and nature of this role remains in question. The tension model of illness on which the Dynamind Technique is based has not been tested with cancer itself to any great degree, but some good results have been achieved with relieving associated symptoms.

The word "cancer" is an intellectual abstraction for a variety of states of tension and disfunction, and the body does not deal with abstractions very well. This means that working directly on the cancer is probably not a viable approach. Therefore, in using Dynamind with people who have cancer it's best to stay with specific symptoms, including feelings and sensations. So you could work on the pain, the nausea, the lack of appetite, the fear of the cancer and its

115

consequences, the anger and helplessness and possibly guilt related to it, etc. You could use the Power Statement to increase circulation, help reduce the size of a tangible tumor, speed up the healing of a wound, instruct the body how to respond to treatment, etc. And you could work on any other fears or angers that the person might have about anything. Remember that Dynamind is designed to relieve tension, and as tension is relieved the body is better able to heal itself.

In my opinion, the approach of trying to find the cause of the cancer is a waste of time because it gets you stuck in the past. The cancer and its symptoms are there right now. Emotional issues exist right now that are maintaining tension right now. Work with the present moment and you'll get better results.

Case O12441-Cancer symptoms: A man of thirty-three had cancer that started on the skin and developed over the thymus, along the spine, and in the brain near the center related to epilepsy. He reported occasional blackouts like an epileptic attack and pain over his thymus area. The session focused on relieving physical tension, anger related to his job, and fear of the illness itself. He felt very relaxed and positive after the session. A few days later he reported that by using Dynamind he was able to abort a blackout attack at the onset. A month later he reported that formerly these attacks had occurred five times a week, and that now he had had only one in four weeks.

Case O35142-Cancer beliefs: In this case the focus was on the feelings about cancer. The client was a middle-aged man with prostate cancer. The feeling he wanted to work on was a strong disbelief that it could be healed, described as a level 8.5 intensity. The first round dealt with the disbelief and the level dropped to 5. Round three was attempted with the same Statement, but the client no longer felt the disbelief. However, the client became aware of a great deal of anger concerning the cancer and the actual round three was done for this anger. Afterward the client said that there was no longer and feeling of disbelief or anger. It is not known what effect this had on his cancer or his cancer treatment.

Case O35143-Fear of cancer: A woman in her late forties had a tumor in her stomach with feelings of fear, anger, and rage at an intensity level of 10. The Statement for the first round was "When I think of the tumor in my stomach I feel fear..." No change. "Fear" was replaced by "powerlessness" for the second round with a slight change. Round three was for disbelief that she could change the condition, but that only lowered the intensity to 9.5. There followed a period of discussion in which she expressed interest in the idea of describing her emotions in terms of patterns instead of feelings. She also agreed to try adding symbols that she could change. The next five rounds dealt with her patterns of resistance, stress, unbelief, anger, and fear, and with each round she formed a symbol of her own and changed it. By the end of the session she described the intensity level, as compared to when she started, as a 1. This is a very good example of how, for certain people, finding the right words to use is the key to progress.

Client Report: I will finish this section with a report provided with the permission of my good friends Don and Mary Kelly. The report was written by Don on his wife's use of the Dynamind Technique during her treatment for cancer. The session with me took place shortly after the couple received the shocking news of the diagnosis from their doctor.

"After that first night, having successfully weathered the 'knock-out punch,' we called our friend and teacher on Kauai, Dr. Serge King, who specializes in the Aloha Spirit and healing using ancient Hawaiian practices. He informed

117

us that he had developed a new procedure called the Dynamind Technique. We flew to see him and had a session right away. He sat across from my wife and asked her if she was having any emotional feelings about her cancer. She couldn't come up with anything at first, and then suddenly she said, 'I feel like I'm ruining our wonderful life.'

"'There's no reason for those feelings of guilt,' he said. 'Let's get rid of them. The Dynamind Technique can make an incredible difference by releasing stored emotions in the space of a minute. You first acknowledge the problem, you relax the mind, you fill the body with breath and energy, and then you use physical touch and specific words to redirect the mind.'

"The session went like this: He said, 'Repeat after me: I'm feeling some guilt about my cancer and that can change. I want that feeling of guilt to go away now.' Mary repeated what he said. 'Now tap your fingers seven times on the breastbone at the center of the chest, then seven times on the area between your left thumb and index finger, now seven times on the right hand, then seven times on the base of the neck. Now take a deep breath, and tell me on a scale of ten, ten being the worst and one being the least, how are you feeling about the guilt?'

"My wife took a deep breath, opened her eyes and said, 'It's at about a seven.'

"'OK' he said. "Let's do it again. Take a deep breath, and do it again.'

"She went through the series again, took a deep breath and said 'It's about a four.'

"'Well then, let's do it once more,' Serge said.

"Mary went through the process one more time and at the end she took a deep breath, and said 'It's gone.'

"'Do you feel anything else? Sadness or anger at the cancer?'

"'Maybe a little fear.' She said.

"'Whenever that comes up, take a deep breath and say, 'I'm feeling a little anxiety and that can change. I want that anxiety to go away now.' Then do the other steps.'

"We were overjoyed to have something positive and constructive to use in our healing. As my wife went through numerous scary tests and treatments, this technique was immensely helpful and gave her the willpower to overcome her challenges. After surgery, when she was feeling nausea, she was able to use the technique to overcome the nausea. She went on to use the technique over and over again, through eight rounds of chemotherapy, seven weeks of radiation, hair loss, weight gain from steroids, and difficult side effects."

Weight Problems

Most weight problems have to do with the difficulty of losing weight. From a purely physical point of view, the solution is very simple. Eat fewer calories or fewer carbohydrates and exercise more. It always works. Except that it doesn't work when emotions are involved. The real problem is not how to lose weight. The real problem is how to deal with the emotions that come up when you try to lose weight. Fat, for instance, may be much more than stored energy. For many people it is stored feelings of anger or fear. Once those feelings are resolved, losing weight is easy. As long as people don't understand the connections between feelings and fat – or don't want to make the connections – obesity will continue and the weight loss industry will keep making lots and lots of money.

Here are a few examples of what might be possible with Dynamind.

Case O39244: An overweight woman of fifty had been unable to lose weight for many, many years. She began a Dynamind session with "My body has a reason to keep me overweight and that can change. I want my body to find a better way to solve my problems." She also did a lot of rounds of Dynamind around issues of resentment and forgiving. According to the case report she lost four kilos (almost nine pounds) without dieting, and she even lost a half kilo (a little over a pound) the day after she ate two big bags of potato chips. No time period was given in the report.

Case O25845: A woman client is using Dynamind for overeating. Her Statement is "I have a pattern of overeating when under stress…" In addition she is consciously relaxing tense muscles in her body before eating. She reports that she is feeling less fear and anger and that she is overeating less.

Case O55546: This therapist reported on a man of thirty-five who has been able to lose a kilo a week (2.2 pounds) without changing his diet or doing more exercise. At the time of the report he had lost four kilos (almost nine pounds) by doing three rounds of Dynamind for weight loss every morning.

Additional Anecdotes

Case OX47-Insomnia: "My upstairs neighbor happened to tell me that she hadn't slept well for over a month because of a backache. I taught her the Dynamind Technique and the next day she looked 100 times better (she'd been looking almost green the day before). She said that she had slept well for the first time in over a month."

Case OX48-Hearing: "I just have to give you an update from the workshop. I was the one with the hearing challenge. Sunday night, after the workshop, I was watching a movie, with my good ear up, and then turned over with my not so good ear up. I automatically reached for the volume control and proceeded to raise the volume. Here comes the shock: Normally, to hear the TV with my right ear up, I have to turn the volume to 59 or 60. Surprise! I could hear fine at 43 and have continued to this day, rarely going beyond that. Some say that this could be a miracle, because over the years, I have had four ear specialists diagnosis my condition. Somehow, I couldn't believe that the Huna healing techniques would last. That is why I waited until now to let you know."

Case OX49-Nail biting: "I have used Dynamind on my 4 year old son to stop him biting his nails once and it worked, he has not bit them in 3 weeks (unbelievable). I thought he would never stop.

p.s. have you heard of anybody using it for golf?"

Case OX50-Surgery: "A few months ago I wrote to you asking for help with healing my ankle. I was having a hard time making progress and you gave me some very good suggestions, including work with Dynamind. I followed your suggestions to the best of my ability, and while I made progress (more than my doctor thought I would), I continued to get the image of something hooked around my ankle bone. No matter how I tried, it just wouldn't budge. I felt like a failure and decided to go ahead and schedule surgery, despite the fact it didn't feel right at that time. I went through with the preliminary stuff even though my inner self did not want this operation and I ended up getting sick a few days before the operation, which was canceled. (Oddly enough, after I told a few friends about the cancellation, they were quite relieved. Apparently they, too, had had strong intuitive messages that that was not the right time.)

Anyway, I hesitated about rescheduling because I still felt like there was something I was doing wrong that was keeping this condition from being cleared up. Finally the pain got to me and I reluctantly rescheduled, but continued to hold out hope for a miracle. I decided to do an all-out, in-depth journey to get the root of the thing. My ankle and I had a heart-to-heart talk and I got the very clear message:

Something is hooked around the ankle bone; have surgery. The rest of me (the part that was not too sanguine about undergoing anesthesia and having to walk on crutches, etc.) was dismayed at the thought of not healing myself. Then I received a very clear message: I am healing myself; I'm just using surgery to do it.

Figuring that I was actually going to go through with it this time, I changed my attitude. For several weeks before the big day, I prepared for surgery by connecting and harmonizing with the spirits of those who were going to be working on me and by doing Dynamind, giving myself suggestions that I was going to tolerate the meds, etc. I even did Dynamind in the waiting room to calm myself down.

The surgery took twice as long as anticipated because -- surprise!-- scar tissue was hooked around the bones and up and over the top of the ankle. The surgeon definitely had not been expecting that.

After the operation, I used Dynamind to control the nausea I felt. Actually, I imagined doing Dynamind because I was so zonked out from the anesthesia that it was too much effort to move my hands. Every time I drifted into consciousness and felt sick I gave myself an affirmation and imagined doing the tapping. I did eventually get a shot to help curb the queasiness, but the attendant told me that I was the only patient who didn't throw up that day.

The drive home, through rush-hour traffic, was challenging nausea-wise until something the nurse had told me finally sunk in. She told me to do deep-breathing in the next 24 hours to dissipate the anesthesia. I gave myself a Dynamind suggestion that I had the power to dissipate the anesthesia easily and pleasantly -- and the nausea disappeared.

I had the stitches removed today (the nurse was surprised at how good it looked (no swelling or anything) and took my first steps. For the first time in one year, I walked without that deep pain in the ankle. So, I'd like to thank you once again for all your help and for sharing Dynamind. It has really helped me so far, and I'm sure it's going to continue to help me in my miraculously fast recovery."

Compound Problems

Some cases are not easy to classify because so many conditions are present at the same time. I will end this chapter with an interesting case that came up very suddenly. It is also a good example of what can be done when a client cannot perform the technique because of his or her condition.

Case OSK51: My wife and I were sitting in the waiting room of a wellness center at a resort waiting for an appointment when a man in his thirties stumbled out of a nearby room and collapsed in a fetal position on a couch across from us. The resident doctor was called in found that the man had very inflamed tonsils that prevented him from swallowing or speaking, a fever, severe cramping in his stomach, and a generalized weakness that made him unable to even sit up. Since we were on an island the doctor was about to order his immediate evacuation by helicopter when the owner of the resort asked if I could try something first. The young doctor reluctantly agreed to give me fifteen minutes "to do my magic."

Well, it wasn't magic, it was Dynamind. I sat next to the man and asked him if he was willing for me to try and help him. He could not speak, but he did nod his head a bit. In a low voice that only he could hear I made SFSs for him, starting with the swelling in his throat. His hands were clutched to his chest, so I could not reach the points properly. Instead, I tapped the backs of his hands and the side of his neck very lightly while I held in my mind the intention of touching the four points of Dynamind. For the Breath I told him what I was doing as I inhaled while touching the top of his head, and exhaled while touching his knee, the lowest point on his body that I could reach comfortably.

I don't know how many rounds we did, but first we cleared the swelling to the point where he could finally swallow, and by that time he was doing the Breath with me. Then we cleared the fever, the cramps, and the weakness. By the time we finished, which was almost exactly fifteen minutes later, he was able to sit up, drink some water, say thanks, and walk to his own apartment on his own. With plenty of water and relaxation exercises by the end of the week he was working and dancing as if nothing had ever happened. And the doctor and I became good friends.

Chapter Five
HEALING ANGER

As noted in the chapter on Dynamind Theory, anger is a fight response, meaning that it is an emotional behavior pattern designed to ward off, push away, change, or eliminate some kind of unwanted experience. In it's natural form, as an expression of discontent common to almost all animals, including humans, it is a kind of warning behavior designed to prevent a potentially dangerous situation from escalating into violent confrontation by reducing stress. It doesn't always work, of course, but it works often enough for it to have become one of our instinctive stress response patterns.

In many human societies and cultures, however, the natural anger response has been refined into a number of unnatural, learned behavior patterns based on a feeling of powerlessness. Whereas natural anger has the survival value of stress reducing behavior, such as when a growling dog warns you that you are invading its eating territory so you will back off, or a dirty look from a friend lets you know that you are carrying a prank too far so that you will stop, unnatural anger only increases stress and often makes some form of violence inevitable. The biggest difference between natural and unnatural anger, though, is that the former operates from a firm sense of personal power, and the latter is born from a sense of helplessness.

Examples of unnatural anger are bitterness, rage, jealousy, resentment, envy, and all forms of suppressed anger. Self criticism and criticism of others can be natural forms of anger when their intended effect is to be a warning of inappropriate behavior or a guide for behavioral change, but they become unnatural when all they do is reduce self esteem and produce humiliation or resentment. Among other anger responses I include grief, guilt, and sadness, because they are forms of resisting experience and because their natural expression leads to positive change. When they become chronic, though, they become unnatural increasers of stress.

There are some schools of anger therapy that promote the open expression of angry feelings as a way of relieving the stress caused by suppressing the feelings or by maintaining them in a chronic way. As a temporary release of the associated tension this can be very therapeutic, but unless the release is followed by mental and emotional behavior change, the therapeutic value will also be temporary. Now I know that there are some therapies that assume anger is like garbage clogging up the emotional plumbing system which needs to be expelled like some kind of hairball, but I heartily disagree with both the assumption and the method. In my experience, anger manifests as a stimulus-response behavior, and not as an accumulation of a vague type of emotional substance. As for the practice of repeatedly discharging the anger in order to get rid of it, it seems to me that the only "benefit" is teaching the client how to get angry at will.

Using my theory of anger and its variations being behavior patterns that can be changed by a combination of tension release and mental change, Dynamind has proven to be highly effective in helping people to become free of their old patterns of unnatural anger, and to restore their sense of personal power and self esteem, all without having to get angry about it.

The following cases involve clients or anecdotes with

anger as the dominant problem, even though fear may be involved as well. They will be divided roughly into those in which self-directed anger is primary, and those in which other-directed anger is more important.

Self-directed Anger

Case ASK01-Guilt: This subject was a woman, probably in her forties, with a feeling of guilt about an undisclosed situation. The round 1 SFS was "When I think about this situation I feel guilt in my bowels..." Her knees now felt weak. Round two dealt with "...weakness in my knees..." Her whole body felt weak. The round three SFS was about her whole body feeling weak, and after this she reported that she felt like there was a dumpling in her throat. This imagery was used in round four as a Symkey to take the dumpling out. There was complete relief from all the feelings of guilt and weakness.

Case A15202-Sadness: This one was quick and simple. A woman in her thirties had been feeling sadness for two months, with an intensity of 9 at the time of the session. Round one was for feeling sad, and the intensity came down to level 5; round two for the same feeling brought to level 3; round three brought the feeling to level 1 and the client was smiling and laughing.

Case A39203-Depression: (SK comment: My interpretation of depression is that it is a symptom of helpless anger, which is why it is included here.) The client, a woman, was feeling tired and emotionally worn out. The round 1 Statement was "I am feeling depressed and that can change; I want to feel real happiness now." When she opened her eyes they were shining and she said she was feeling great and began smiling.

Case A71204-Self blame: A woman client felt like something was wrong with her. She blamed herself for not being good enough, for not feeling loved, for being depressed, and for being afraid that God did not love her.

The round 1 SFS was "I have a problem with always feeling that there's something wrong with me..." Her breathing was better and she had a warm and good feeling in her body, but a slightly uncomfortable sensation in her throat. The therapist suggested an emotional assumption and the round two SFS was "I have a problem with holding blame in my throat..." This revealed a soreness in her solar plexus, which the client described as a "raw" feeling. Round three was for the raw feeling, and the client reported that "The rawness is now just in one very small spot, and now it's all gone."

The client wanted to continue, so the round four SFS was "I have a problem with holding anger in my solar plexus..." The client said, "It feels like it's breaking up, I see clouds moving away, the sun is shining." Round five used the same Statement and the client's imagery as a Symkey, allowing the clouds to rain if needed, lightning to flash if needed, and to let the sun grow bigger and brighter. The client's response to this was "I see beautiful colors; I feel happy, harmonious and energized."

The session ended with six rounds of Power Statements on the power to feel happy, harmonious, energized and loved. At the end the client said, "That was incredible!"

Case A12405-Low self esteem: A woman of thirty-three had difficulty with self esteem because she didn't believe in herself. She had spent twelve years in psychotherapy and had tried to commit suicide twice. She reported having felt anger and fear since childhood. The intensity at the time of the session was level 10.

Round 1: "I have fear in my body..." Her breathing became deeper and she had tears in her eyes.

128

Round 2: "I have anger in my body…" More tears, but she had more relaxation in her chest.

Round 3: "I have the Power to like myself, yes I can, make it happen, make it so." She stood up and shouted out, "I love myself, I like myself! Where are all the men? I want to show myself to the world!" The intensity level at this point was 0 and she had a very grateful feeling.

Case A12406-Pressure to be perfect: The client was a woman of forty-nine and mother of four children. She had feelings of stress from her family, and she felt that she was the only person responsible for the happiness and unhappiness of the family. She said that whenever she needed her husband, he was not present. Since childhood she had also felt pressure from her mother to be a perfect woman. The sensation of feeling pressure was at a level 8, and the feeling of anger was at level 9

Round 1: "I have a feeling of pressure in my whole body…" The pressure feeling went down to level 4.

Round 2: "I still feel pressure and tension in some parts of my body…" The pressure feeling went to level 0 and a there were alot of tears.

Round 3: "I have anger in my body…" The anger went to level 3.

Round 4: "I have anger in my heart when I think on my Husband…" The anger went to level 1.

Round 5: "I still have anger and tension in my heart when I think about my husband…" The intensity of the anger was at level 0. The client was crying, but she felt more relaxed, and she also had a feeling of warmth and love inside her body.

Case A69607-Self anger: The client was a man of forty-five, often in trouble at work because of his tempermental and flamboyant behavior. He was feeling some anger at his co-workers because of their complaints, but mostly anger at himself for causing the problem. The intensity of feeling was level 8.

Round 1: "When I'm thinking about the people in my environment and about the situations in which I'm not behaving well, I'm feeling excluded and disapproved, and that can change. I want to behave correctly and I want people to like me and love me. Please, make it happen, make it so." He felt much better after this, and he realized that he had been telling himself that people didn't like him. His feelings were now at level 4.

Round 2: The same SFS. "I feel much better. I'm sure I'll be able to behave myself as I'm imagining." The feeling was at level 2. He was advised to continue Dynamind when the angry feelings arose.

Feedback from the client after two weeks: "I've succeeded in changing my behaviour and the best thing is, it has been confirmed by my co-workers."

Case A25808-Guilt: A woman, age seventy-six, was having trouble getting over the loss of her boyfriend of two years who had died about a year before. She was very depressed at the time of the session, but she wanted to work on the guilt, even though she had some reservations about the process. Her intensity level was 8.

Round 1: "I feel anger at myself for not monitoring my boyfriend's heart condition better..." The level went down to 4, whereupon she wanted to discredit the whole thing by saying, "Of course it's less; I'm trying to make it less." The therapist gave her some examples of her own experience with Dynamind and got the client to agree that if she felt better she'd just accept it.

Round 2: "I feel disappointed in myself for not monitoring my boyfriend's heart condition better..." The sensation of guilt went to zero. She then decided to work on how she didn't even really want to get out of bed in the morning.

Round 3: "I don't feel like getting out of bed in the morning..."

Round 4: The same. Now the client said that she could picture herself getting up and feeling brighter. So the therapist led her in some affirmative statements to that effect and she left feeling better.

She called the therapist later to say she felt much calmer than she had in a very long time after the session and that she felt even better the next day.

Case A69209-Regret: An elderly man had had negative thoughts about himself for some time. He spoke to the therapist about the many things he had not done in his life. Thinking of all the missed opportunities made him feel bad and worthless. The level of this feeling was 8-9.

Round 1: "When I think of my life I remember the many things that I didn't do and feel bad..."

Round 2: "When I look at my life I have the feeling of being a loser..."

Round 3: "I think of myself with anger..."

Round 4: "I am angry at myself..."

Now he felt better. He recognized that "it had just been a feeling." He planned to make a list of all the good things he had achieved in his life. He said he was quite confident that "it wasn't for nothing."

Case A69210-Self criticism: A middle-aged woman was having trouble at work. She said she felt like the worst idiot, she had been crying, and she felt bad and depressed. With the help of the therapist she tried at first to relieve the tension in her head and the tension in her breast, with little success. Then they worked on her behavior toward herself.

Round 1: "When I think of my job, I criticise myself badly..."

Round 2: "When I am criticised I feel tension in my body…"
The mentioning of her criticising at first brought even more tension, but after a few repetitions the tension vanished completely. She said she felt really good and appreciated.

Case AX11-Self criticism in sports: "A friend of mine is a member of a fencing-club. As they had a tournament recently she was very successful, beating all concurrents until she found herself in the finals. There her success continued, giving her a comfortable advantage. But then things changed, and she lost one point after the other, getting more and more nervous and angry. Finally the score was even and the next point was to decide about the winner of the tournament. At that time she remembered Dynamind. The simple thought of it relaxed her, and she mentally said, "I am angry about myself and this can change. I want this problem to go away!" She did the Breath with a deep sigh, concentrated on her game, and won the last point and the entire tournament."

Case AX12-Frustration: "We had a visit from friends who reported the following experience. They had been in church for the service of Easter night, an event full of ritual and music. The man said he was very reluctant at first, and when the unprofessional sermon frustrated him to extremes, he thought about leaving the church right away. But he remained and did Dynamind instead. The experience changed completely. It was no longer boring, it was wonderful to him, and towards the end he had a deep spiritual experience of unity (he felt like a drop relaxing into the ocean). He went home totally happy and with a feeling of enlightenment.

Case A41913-Shame: The client was a woman who was very uncomfortable with her sexuality. Just talking about it made her giggle, so the therapist assumed that there might be feelings of guilt, shame, and fear associated with sexuality. The client agreed to work on those assumptions.

Round 1: "When I think about my sexuality I feel fear and that can change…" Then a Power Statement about it being okay to think about sex was added. After this she didn't giggle but still felt some slight embarrassment.

Round 2: "When I think about my sexuality I feel embarrassed…" A Power Statement was added and there were no more adverse feelings.

Case A36114-Abstract anger: A woman, forty, was angry because "in the world there is so much chaos." She wanted the world to be at peace, but the size of the problem made her even more upset.

Round 1: "I am restless and that can change…" She felt more peaceful.

Round 2: "I want to have peace and that is good. Make it happen, make it so." She was more calm

Round 3: "I live in peace…" She felt enthusiasm.

Round 4: "My life is full of enthusiasm…"

Round 5: "I`m angry that I cannot live my enthusiasm in the world of chaos and that can change…" She felt that her heart was jumping.

Round 6: "I am living my enthusiasm and that is good…"

The woman was lauphing and the session ended.

Case A36115-Guilt: A woman in her thirties had ended a personal partnership with a man two years previously and she still had many feelings of guilt and unhappiness.

Round 1: "I`m feeling guilty that I have finished our partnership…" She became aware that she felt responsible for the man's happiness.

Round 2: "I feel responsible for this man's happiness…" She became aware that she also felt responsible for her father's happiness.

Round 3: "I feel responsible for my father's happiness..." She felt doubt that this was not true.

Round 4: "I have doubt that this can change..." The doubt went away, but she felt a heavy, painful feeling like a yoke around her shoulders.

Round 5: "I feel a yoke around my shoulders..."

Round 6: Same Statement, plus an image of an angel who took off the yoke and carried it away. Afterward, the yoke was still there, but it was lighter.

Round 7: Same SFS plus an image of more angel helpers. The yoke and the pain were gone. She began crying.

Rounds 8-11 were Power Statements for freedom, happiness and personal power, and at the end she felt she had more power and courage to lead her own life.

Case A13116-Low self esteem: The client was a highly skilled, multi-talented woman therapist in her forties who had been in psychotherapy for some time because her life had been painful, dissatisfying, and "stuck" in many ways.

In particular she had serious problems with decision-making and relationships, and she was quite overweight. This session was particularly interesting because of the elaborate, profound, work she did with the imagery that developed for her. The level of intensity of her feelings of unhappiness was 9-10.

Round 1: "I have believed that I am innately incompetent, and this can change. I want to know and recognize my own intelligence and competency." After the Breath a pressure came up in her forehead.

Round 2: Same Statement (SST). The therapist suggested that she make that pressure into a symbol, and change it as needed. "It is a bright sun shining as though it was under cloud cover."

Round 3: SST. The client enhanced the image and reported, "It opened up more. There ís a sensation spreading across my forehead." She then made motions of moving energy with her hands across her forehead to the sides, through her hair. "It feels as though the sun is mostly shining, except for one hold-back area in the back on the right side. There ís a cloud obscuring part of the sun."

Round 4: SST. The pressure lifted upward and became like a tight helmet or a tight hat. "The cloud is bigger now, and the sun is smaller, farther away. Breath or wind needs to blow it away." (So she blew it away.) "Now hooks are stuck in my forehead above eyebrows. I'm putting a protective jelly around the hook so that when the hook is removed, it won't hurt. Now I'm taking out the left hook. Now I'm filling the space in with positive, yellow energy, then blue." (She was sending this positive energy in with her fingers on her face.) "The fingers on my face are really hot." (She left them in place for some time.) "Now I'm going over to work on the other one. This one goes much deeper, like it's wrapped down and around my inner ear. Something is loosening up, like a knot being untied, or untangled. Now the main body of the hook is starting to come out." (She verified that she had put protective jelly around this one, too. It came out sharply, with a breath.) "There ís an itching in my inner ear. It ís the clearing process."

Since the clearing wasn't happening very quickly, the therapist suggested that the client do some Toning, which the woman used with her own clients. She did so, and it finally cleared. (SK note: "Toning" is a type of therapy in which vocal sounds are directed toward specific locations on the body, usually chakra points) "The sun ís back to being a big sun. There ís only one little dark space left." The therapist suggested that the client ask the dark space what it was or what message it had. Tears came up immediately and she said, "A wave of grief about my Dad."

Round 5: "In the past I've believed I had to accept and take on my father's perception of who I am and how the world works, and that can change. I want to know and accept my own true belief of who I am and how the world works, and release the disfunctional belief that that's who I am and how the world works, and replace it with my own true knowledge." The result of this round was reported by the client as "A big internal shift. The helmet sensation is almost gone and the sun is bigger and brighter, but there is one piece remaining, right at the crown." The therapist suggested she focus on that. "The message is, `God is not Dad!'" She repeated that declaration, then removed it from the top of her head with her hands. There was an effect at the back of her head, which she breathed through, then a quick pull-out. After some more positive affirmations and some piko-piko breathing to clear up a tingling in her legs she reported that her initial problem level was down to 0.

Case A13117-Perfectionism: The client was a male accountant whose obsession with perfection was causing him serious personal and business difficulties. The main problem was a belief that not being perfect made him a bad person. Despite his typical resistance to alternative therapies, he agreed to proceed. The therapist suggested that the Statement be put into the past tense. The problem level was 9.

Round 1: "I have believed that every error I made meant that I was a bad person, so I had to review everything I did and everything my assistant did to make sure I caught any errors and got the client all the tax breaks possible, and this can change. I want to be able to say to a client who has found an error, 'Mr. Client, my error rate is the lowest in the business, but the fact that we use a phrase like error rate means that some errors do happen, and I'm sorry one of our infrequent errors happened to you. If we got our error rate to zero, we would have to charge over $1000 for each return, and you know I'm not charging you that now." After the first round of Dynamind, he was visibly changed, and he reported that he was already at a 1.5. The therapist was very surprised at this, but noted that he was "really very present for the process, with a very strong focus." The client chose to do the same process again, and he was instructed to use Dynamind daily to reinforce the results of the current session.

Later, he said, "I feel a lot more energy now! I'm going to make some calls right away to tell some clients their returns will be late as a result of my decision to not work all night for the next several nights, and also to go running, which makes me feel good, rather than just stay at my desk!"

From the therapist: "I feel that a huge breakthrough was made for this person today, because it may not only remove a terrible burden of guilt, but also open him to further healing in the future."

Case A35118-Self reproach: This male, Native American client in his forties was angry with himself after breaking up with his partner. He was particularly angry at not being more like the Buddha, Mother Theresa or Jesus, and with the anger of many lifetimes because of his heritage as a Native American. The issue of anger had been ongoing, and the intensity level at the time of the session was 7. The Dynamind Destresser was used first.

Round 1: "I have a feeling of anger…" The anger with himself moved from 7 to 2 and was felt "behind my heart." Now he felt a sense of cloudiness in his head due to a hangover, so the next round addressed that problem.

Round 2: "I have a feeling of cloudiness in my head…" The sense of cloudiness in his head moved to a level 2 and he did this two more times as he felt it again later in the session.

Of interest is the fact that this Native American client customized the ritual of Dynamind by adding elements from his cultural heritage. He did the Breath from Wakan Tanka or Sky Father to Earth Mother; he did the Touch with a peace pipe and chanted for a count of seven at each point; and he did a Dynamind Developer Statement to "Be as confident as Brother Eagle; as wise as Brother Wolf." The session ended with the Dynamind Toner. At the beginning of the session his face was puffy and uneven. By the end of the session the puffiness had disappeared and his mouth became even. In addition, he spoke with smiles and laughter; said that he felt empowered and less helpless; and declared that he was happy to acknowledge his anger and to change it with Dynamind.

Case A35119-Powerlessness: The client was a woman in her late forties. Her presenting problem was that she had a tumor in her stomach and felt anger, rage, and fear with an intensity level of 10. Fear was addressed first, but proved not to be the real problem.

Round 1: "When I think of the tumor in my stomach I feel fear and that can change..." Still at level 10.

Round 2: SFS for powerlessness. The result was a small change to 9-10.

Round 3: "When I think of the tumor in my stomach I don't believe that I can change it..." Another small change to level 9.5.

There followed some discussion about how she needs to know why something happened before she can change it. From the beginning of the session she also had difficulty with the word "feeling." After some more discussion the client agreed to suspend disbelief and work with symbols and to change the patterns. Everything moved quickly after that because the way was found to fit the session to the client's needs.

Round 4: "I have the pattern of being powerless and this can change…" She worked on her own making the symbol and changing it until it felt right. She let the therapist know when she was ready to move on, and she changed the Statements herself.

Round 5: "I have the pattern of resistance and that can change…" She inserted her own Symkey during this round, and during all subsequent rounds.

Round 6: I have the pattern of stress and that can change…" Inserted Symkey.

Round 7: "I have the pattern of unbelief and that can change…" Inserted Symkey.

Round 8: "I have the pattern of anger and that can change…" Inserted Symkey.

Round 9: "I have the pattern of fear and that can change…" Inserted Symkey"

The session ended with a Dynamind Toner and Developer. At the end of the session the intensity level had moved from 10 to 1 and she looked like a different person. She wore a Cheshire Cat smile and was very happy and much more relaxed.

Case A35120-Self reproach: A woman in her forties felt incompetent. She was having problems with her husband and felt that she had failed in some way. She described her feeling about the current issue as being at a level 8.

Round 1: "I have feelings of grief, sadness and regret…" Level 5.

Round 2: Same statement Level 5.

Round 3: Same statement plus a Symkey of a little girl scared and beaten up, and a feeling that there was nothing to protect the little girl. The client changed the symbol to introduce a genie threatening the other, unnamed person. The scared feeling stopped and the original problem went to level 4.

Round 4: "I have the feeling that everything is my fault…" The Symkey used was that of a little girl feeling rotten and beating her self up mentally. This was changed to giving gifts to herself, such as a bubble bath, toys, a candle, flowers, cake, and chocolate. This felt good.

Over the course of the session the intensity level moved from 8 to +1. The client stated, "I felt that it is so easy to feel good and change our minds." She smiled and laughed and hugged the therapist. She treated herself to a chocolate ice cream afterwards.

Case AX21-Unhappiness: "When I just feel unhappy or stressed without knowing exactly what the problem is, I simply start the first round of Dynamind with "I feel stressed and that can change…" Then there is already a release of tension so that I know can feel a distinct emotion like anger which I can work on. After my first experience of that kind I realised that this situation actually indicates a serious state of stress when the body has closed itself away from all the bothering emotions with the result that I feel very separated from myself. Before using Dynamind it often took a long time to recover and the danger of an escalation was also there. But now I know how to help myself instantly and that's great!"

Case AX22-Low self esteem: "I wanted to share with you the latest results I am getting from doing the Dynamind process the other day for my self-esteem issues. First of all, I am so glad that I now see things for what they really are, or the things that have been taking place in my life over the past few days would have destroyed me. This past week I have been feeling an overpowering sense of unrest at work. I felt like nothing I did was right or good enough, that I was letting everyone down, and I just couldn't motivate myself to fix all this. So then my boss told me that the owner of the company was unhappy with my work. In the past this would have destroyed me. Imagine how it feels to know that, even though you are working like crazy and dealing with family and money problems, it's not good enough. This has always struck me right at my heart and soul, making me feel that who I am is not good enough. With the help of Dynamind I suddenly realized that I have to learn to love myself for who I am, not letting other's opinions of me be what makes me whole, or not. Now, I must say, I am quite amazed at my strength in dealing with this. As I have said, in the not-too-distant past, this would have destroyed me. What power we truly have, and what amazing results come from the Dynamind technique."

Other-directed Anger

Case ASK23-Betrayal: The subject was a man in his thirties who felt that his feelings about something that happened when he was very young were interfering with his present success. Specifically, it concerned the fact that his mother had left the household when he was about seven, and he was angry with her "for having betrayed him."

The first round was done with an SFS for the feeling of betrayal that was in his chest. This resulted in a symptom shift to a feeling of weakness in his legs in addition to the feeling of unhappiness in his heart. At this point I taught him my "Skinny Description" technique, because I could see that the word "betrayal" was itself causing a lot of stress. In this technique I have the subject or client describe a past event in a factual way without any adjectives. After a few tries the man was able to describe the event as one in which "My mother left home and I didn't know why." This led to an awareness that his real unhappiness came from her lack of attention to him.

Round two used the SFS "I feel unhappy in my heart

because my mother did not give me enough attention..."
The anger was gone, and replaced by another realization.

The SFS for round three was "I was afraid because my mother was afraid..." All feelings of anger, resentment and sadness were gone and he felt ready to move forward with his career.

Case A15224-Rage: The client was a woman in her forties with rage at having been abused by her father all her life. The intensity level at the time of the sesion was 10+. Round one used an SFS for rage felt in her solar plexus. When the round started she thought she would cry, but at the end of the round she was rolling on the floor laughing, even though the rage that had been centered in her solar plexus moved to her throat at a level 2. Although the client felt much better, she did not want to do any more Dynamind because this was done during a group therapy session, but promised to do it on her own. In a follow-up one week later the client seemed like a different person, smiling and laughing, and she appeared to be coping with problems in a positive and relaxed way. She said the rage went out through her eyes.

Case A15225: A woman in her forties was upset at being falsely accused of something at work. The first round was an SFS for being upset, and afterward she felt more centered. Round two was done for feeling upset in her solar plexus, and she felt nervous afterward. Round three was for fear and included a Symkey image: "I have a hard, brown, knobbly knot weighing 2 ounces in my solar plexus. I watch it unknot and leave my body" and after she felt a bit depleted. The client continued on her own and two days later reported feeling much better.

Case A12426-Anger at a divorce: A woman of fifty-four came to the session with tears running down her face, because she had just received final divorce papers that morning. All the angry feelings from the last twenty-six years came up, as well as feelings about the anger she got from her husband. She felt pain in her lower back and in her right sciatic nerve. First, the therapist led her through five minutes of Dynamind rounds using the Blanket Forgiveness phrase "Whatever my husband did I forgive it completely and it doesn't matter any more" and the pain was gone. Then more rounds were done to clear anger, fear, tension, and doubt. The session ended with the Power Statement "My body has the power to live in peace and happiness for the rest of my life, yes it does. I have the Power to live in peace and happiness, too." Her tears stopped and she smiled, hugged the therapist, and said that she felt much better.

Case A12427-Anger at a husband: The client was a woman of sixty who said she didn't love her husband any longer and felt that there must be a better lover for her somewhere, because she didn't feel anything when she was touched by her husband. The feeling of not loving her husband was at a level 9.

Round 1: "There is a feeling deep inside me that I do not love my husband..." Level 5.

Round 2: There is fear in some parts of my body and my mind because this feeling..." Level 3 with a lot of tears.

At this point the therapist guided the client through five minutes of rounds using the Blanket Forgiveness Statement for the woman's feelings about herself. This resulted in a lot of tears and loud crying from deep inside. After this the client said that she realized that her husband was the best lover she had had for a long time. She was so happy, but sad, too, because she was afraid it might be too late for she and her husband to become a good couple. The therapist gave her some advice on repairing relationships and the final feeling level was 0.

Case A69628-Anger at work: The client was a man of forty-five who was being treated badly by his foreman whenver no one else was around. He felt like he was under attack and his anger level was 9.

Round 1: "When I'm thinking about my foreman, I'm feeling sorrowful and injured, and that can change. I want these bad feelings to disappear, and the relationship between my foreman and me to become harmonious. Please, make it happen, make it so." The client's face became more relaxed, and he said, "I feel better." Level 5.

Round 2: SST plus "I forgive you, foreman, no matter in which context it may be. Please make it happen, make it so." When the round was over the client said, "My feelings have never been so good before, when I'm thinking about my foreman." Level 1 to 2.

Feedback after two weeks: "The cooperation with my foreman is much better now. We even can have a normal conversation, which wasn't possible before."

Case A69629-Anger at a relative: A woman in her eighties appeared tired and tense because her daughter-in-law was meddling in her financial affairs. The client was so angry and furious about it that she couldn't even sleep. The anger intensity was level 7.

Round 1: "When I'm thinking about my daughter-in-law I'm angry and in a rage..." The anger level dropped to 4 and the client raised her eyebrows and looked very surprised as she felt the change.

Round 2: "When I'm thinking about my daughter-in-law, I'm still feeling a bit of rage and anger..." After this round the client said, "I'm feeling much lighter in my head," and she gave the anger a level 1-2.

Round 3: The same. "My head feels very light, and when I'm thinking about my daughter-in-law it is like I'm thinking about my neighbour." At the end of the session the therapist had the impression that the client was looking much younger.

Case A69630-Anger at a father: The client was a single man of thirty-eight. The problem was that whenever he thought about his father, negative memories and impressions came up which still made him furious and angry. These feelings were at level 9 when the session began.

Round 1: "When I'm thinking about my father I'm getting furious and angry, and that can change. When I'm thinking about my father I want to feel free and relaxed. Please make the energy between my father and me harmonious." After this round the client said, "I'm feeling freer, and I don't feel the heat coming up anymore." Level 5.

Before doing the next round the therapist asked the client to describe three situations in which he had enjoyed thinking about his father. The client's face brightened as he told about the day he got his bicycle, about the tours he'd made with his father, and about the times when he played with his father and a toy train.

Round 2: Same Statement as Round 1. "I'm feeling better, but I'm also having a funny feeling that I can't describe." The anger level was now at 2.

The therapist recommended that the client make a list at home of seven to ten pleasant memories about his father, and as soon as disagreeable feelings appeared, to repeat the Dynamind as he had just learned it. Afterwards, he could look at the list of good memories and read it loudly to himself.

Feedback after three weeks. "I've done Dynamind several times and then I've read seven nice memories loudly for myself. The emotional relationship to my father has become so much better that I'm planning to visit him soon.

Case A25831-Anger at a business partner: The client was a woman whose business establishment had recently burned down, prompting her and her business partner to dissolve their partnership, something the client

function this weekend…" Whereupon the client realized that she really didn't want to get rid of her anger, because she felt like it was a necessary protection. After some discussion the client recognized that she felt guilty that she hadn't seen this lawsuit coming and protected her family better.

Round 2: "When I think about this situation I feel guilty…" It lessened. This recognition of guilt and self-blame was a surprise and very significant to her.

Round 3: "I have the power to be confident, comfortable and totally centered this weekend…"

The client called back on Monday and reported that the weekend went very well. She kept calm and collected, didn't cause a scene and actually enjoyed the function. She also reported that she used the power statement with the Dynamind quite a lot and credited that and the rest of the work with the therapist for making the weekend a success.

Case A69233-Anger at work: The client was a woman in her forties having trouble at her workplace and therefore having stomach pain. She gave the whole problem a level 9.5.

Round 1: "When I think of certain persons, I feel awfully bad in my stomach…" Level 8.

Round 2: "When I think of these persons, I stop feeling good…" Level 7.

Round 3: "Thinking of the situation gives me a feeling of being under attack and that can change. I am immune against all kinds of personal attack and intimidation." Level 3.

Round 4: "I have a problem with intrigues and that can change. I let go of all affinity with intrigues. This is no longer a topic of interest for me." Level 1.

The woman reported later that the morning after the session she had a tremendous headache, which she was able to resolve on her own with Dynamind as she had learned it in the session.

Case A69234-Anger at friends: A young woman had been feeling anger and disappointment for the last few weeks about her relationship with some friends. Level 7.5.

Round 1: "When I think of these girlfriends, I feel anger toward them…"

Round 2: "I feel disappointment with my friends…"

Round 3: "I'm really pissed off at my friends…"

After that, she said she felt "super". She said she could now imagine approaching new friends. Actually, she said, she didn't have very much feeling left towards her old friends.

Case A41935-Anger at the past: The client was a woman who felt anger and resentment about a traumatic event that had happened a few years ago.

Round 1: "When I think about this event I feel anger and resentment, and that can change…" This was followed by a Power Statement to boost her confidence. A Symkey was also used in which she asked an Elf friend to remove the feeling which looked to her like black smoke. At the end of the round she noticed tension in her jaw.

Round 2: "When I think about this event I feel tension in my jaw…" No tension in the jaw, but tension in the throat.

Round 3: "When I think about this event I feel tension in my throat…" Now there was a sense of sadness.

Round 4: "When I think about this event I feel sad…" Power statment. Now she noticed tension in her shoulders.

Round 5: "When I think about this event I feel tension in my shoulders…" The shoulder tension was cleared.

The client reported that two days later that while thinking about the event she did not have any tension or adverse feelings.

Case A36136-Anger at work: A woman in her forties had a dispute with a colleague at work about the purchase of needed equipment.

Round 1: "When I think about this problem I feel tension in my chest…" She became aware of tension in her neck.

Round 2: "I have a tension in my neck…" The tension in her neck eased a bit, and she became more aware of the anger.

Round 3: "I feel anger toward my colleage…"

Rounds 4-6 consisted of Power Statements affirming positive expectations concerning the situation, and by the end of the session the tension in her neck was only a little and she was laughing and feeling lighter.

Case A35137-General anger: The client was a woman in her forties with anger at level 8. No reason for the anger was given.

Round 1: "I have a feeling of anger…" The client felt a need to melt the anger.

Round 2: "I feel that anger will serve me, and that can change. I acknowledge anger, but don't retain it." A Symkey was added of the client expressing anger by kicking and stomping and saying, "They can't walk over me." A voice from someone else said, "I hear you," and the person in the image took off their cap. The anger level moved to a 2 and the client felt a great deal of happiness.

Chapter Six
HEALING FEAR

We do not inherit fear from our ancestors. It is not an instinctive reaction, nor is it necesary for survival. Caution, yes; recognition of potential danger, yes; but not fear. We have to be taught how to be afraid.

I remember when I was a young boy watching my younger sister walk down a hallway in our home while smashing spiders on the wall with her hand. I thought it was disgusting, my sister thought it was fun, my Mom thought it was horrifying. I can still hear her screams when she saw my sister happily diminishing the spider population, and I remember how quickly my sister changed her attitude and behavior toward spiders after only one intensive spiders-are-awful-be-afraid-of-them training session.

One minute we can be fearless, and in the next we can learn to be fearful. For the moment let's put aside the question of whether fear has any value. The issue at hand is whether it is inborn or acquired behavior.

Here is another example, opposite to the one above. On a sunny day on a broad beach in Africa, when the ocean was like a calm lake, I noticed that my four-year-old and seven-year-old sons were having fun in the water, and my three-year-old son was having fun on the sand. No problem with that, except that I also noticed how he scampered out of the way every time the smallest wavelet came within two feet of him. This looked like a job for "Parentman!"

I picked up my three-year-old, talked to him soothingly, and carried him a few steps toward the water. He immediately tried to squirm out of my arms, even though the water was only around my ankles. He was clearly afraid, so I stopped, calmed him down, and took a few more steps forward. Of course, he reacted in the same way. Very slowly and gently, using a classic psychological method of desensitization, I was able to get him to accept being in the water ankle deep, waist deep, chest deep, and, finally, we even ducked under the water together. After that I returned him to shore and let him develop his own relationship to the ocean. Today my youngest son is a US Navy Seal.

One more example to illustrate my point. During a workshop on the Dynamind Technique I had a young woman on stage who said she was afraid of water. We further refined that to be a state of paralyzing panic when facing a swimming pool. Even further refinement produced the interesting discovery that the panic occured only when the pool was closer than two meters, more than one meter wide, and the color of the water was blue. In fact, regardless of the size or proximity of the pool, the panic disappeared if the color of the water was green.

In the first example above, my sister had no fear of spiders until she was taught to be afraid by our mother. Her first reaction to them was the instinctive one. In the second example, my son was afraid of the ocean, not the water itself. I know this because I had seen him happily splashing bath water all over on numerous occasions. I have no idea what event taught him to be afraid - and he doesn't remember - but his ability to get rid of the fear in such a short time definitely indicates a learned behavior and not an instinctive one. And in the last example, the fact that so many specific conditions had to be met before the debilitating fear occured is indicative of learned behavior as well.

This would be a good time to define what I mean by "instinctive" behavior, because many people confuse it with "automatic" behavior. Behavior is automatic when you have learned it so well you don't have to think about it anymore. It is basically a stimulus response like Pavlov's dog salivating at the ringing of a bell. For many people, riding a bicycle, using silverware, reacting with fear to specific events, or getting cold symptoms when you get your feet wet in street shoes, but not in beach sandals, are common examples of automatic behavior. Such behavior is linked closely to individual experience and cultural expectations.

Instinctive behavior, on the other hand, is common to all humans and not dependent on individual experience or culture. Breathing is instinctive; breathing rates are learned. Eating is instinctive; food choices are learned. The urges to get warm when you are cold, get cool when you are hot, seek security when you feel insecure, or move toward or repeat pleasurable experiences, and move away from or avoid unpleasant or painful experiences are all part of humanity's repertoire of instinctive behaviors. As mentioned in the last chapter, even the fight reaction of anger to a threat is instinctive, as is the flight reaction of trying to avoid it. Flight, however, does not require fear. If you like, we could give the name "natural fear" to instinctive behavior that involves avoiding danger, but I prefer to think of that as common sense.

Another important difference between instinctive and learnied behaviors is that learned behaviors, automatic or not, are capable of being unlearned or modified very quickly, whereas instinctive behaviors can only be suppressed, amplified, or redirected.

It is a fact, supported by abundant research, experiments and experience, that fears can be unlearned, often quickly, without suppression, amplification or redirection. This alone puts them into the learned behavior category.

Part of the misunderstanding about fear comes from early experiments in which babies were tossed into the air and observations were made of their behavior. The instinctive reaction of seeking a connection to something secure was interpreted as an expression of fear. Actually, as long as you don't drop them, some babies get immense enjoyment from being tossed into the air.

"As long as you don't drop them." This brings up the subject of how fear gets learned in the first place. For that to happen, three vital factors must be present: self-doubt, a memory of pain, and an expectation of pain.

Self-doubt is the most important factor, for without it fear doesn't occur. Self-doubt is also learned behavior, but it can be learned while you are still a fetus. Basically, self-doubt is born when an individual interprets a feeling or sensation as meaning that one has lost contact with a source of power or love. To the degree that this interpretation is repeated with similar feelings or sensations it becomes learned and automatic behavior.

Memories of some kind of pain are present in everyone, but everyone is not affected by them in the same way. Fear is born - and eventually learned - when self-doubt is present at the time a painful experience occurs because, due to the self-doubt, an expectation of pain arises under any stimulus that resembles the original pain. When I was about seven-years-old I was playing with some friends and we decided to climb a tree and jump off a large branch. The other boys did it without a problem. They didn't have any self-doubt, at least in relation to jumping out of trees, so that even if they had gotten hurt in the past from leaping off a branch they had no expectation of pain from doing it again. I, however, had sufficient self-doubt, and a memory of a previous painful fall not related to trees, so that I crouched on the branch, frozen with fear, for a very long time. The other boys simply crawled around me and jumped to their heart's content. At long last I suppressed my fear, gathered my courage, and leaped into the unknown - it was my first experience of branch-jumping. Fortunately, I had a good landing and it was so much fun I did it over and over, unlearning my fear in the process.

One of the last sentences in the previous paragraph reminds me of another aspect of fear that needs clarification, the so-called "fear of the unknown." Actually, there is no such thing. It's always a fear of the known. Or, rather, a fear of not knowing. If we experience something truly unknown we will either be curious or we will ignore it. Fear only arises in this case when a new experience reminds us of a previous painful experience and we have an expectation of another painful experience because we don't know what to do.

Here is the moral of the story. It doesn't matter if we have self-doubt, or painful memories, or fear of anything whatsoever. We learned how to act one way; we can teach ourselves how to act differently. Self-doubt can be erased by teaching ourselves - over and over and over again - to trust in ourselves and/or in a higher power. To trust, not that nothing bad will ever happen, but that whatever happens we will be able to cope with it, and that more good things will happen than bad. How do we know? We don't. The future is never fixed, but now is the moment of power. What we do and how we think in the present moment may not control the future, but it has more influence on the future than anything else. There is no fear without self-doubt. Self-doubt begins with a decision. It can end with a decision, too.

The Many Faces Of Fear

There are many varieties of fear, ranging from

mild uncertainty to full-blown, paralyzing terror. The cases presented below will be organized roughly into categories of intensity. The varieties of lesser intensity, however, may be just as debilitating to one individual as more intense forms might to another, so no judgment as to importance is implied by the order of the categories.

As a reminder, "SFS" means "Standard Format Statement," meaning one that follows the form "I have a problem and that can change. I want the problem to go away." And a "Symkey" is a symbolic image generally starting as a representation of a problem, and then altered in some way to produce a change in a feeling or symptom. Also, a Power Statement is a reinforcing affirmation that follows the form "I have the power to do something, yes I do. Make it happen, make it so." Deviations from these forms are not only permitted, they are encouraged when they help a person to make a change more easily. Finally, although rarely mentioned, every round of Dynamind described is accompanied by the Touch and the Breath.

Self Doubt

Often described as a lack of confidence, this kind of fear is most frequently based on a fear of criticism, which is essentially a fear of rejection and disconnection. The first case in this section makes this very clear.

Case FSK01-Fear of being criticized: A woman came on stage and admitted to being afraid of a particular, critical person.

Round 1: "When I think of this critical person I feel weak in my chest…" She felt stronger in the chest, but her legs were trembling.

Round 2: "I feel trembling in my legs…" She felt calmed down and no longer afraid.

Case F71202-Lack of confidence: The client was

a man who wanted to work on self-confidence.

Round 1: An SFS for confidence plus a Symkey suggested by the therapist of the client in posture of self confidence. The man did not like the image.

Round 2: The same SFS plus a Symkey superimposing someone already confident (The man chose God).

Round 3: The same SFS with the Symkey made stronger.

Round 4: The SFS with an image/feeling of concrete energy pouring into his physical, emotional, mental and spiritual bodies, including his bones.

Round 5: The Power Statement "I am loved, I always have been loved, I always will be loved, and every day in every way this love keeps growing." After this round the man said, "I feel wonderful. At peace, calm and serene."

Case F12403-Fear of making decisions: A woman of forty-eight had so much self doubt that her husband left her six months ago because he said he could not live with her craziness any longer. The general problem was her difficulty in making decisions, and the specific problem was her fear about making the wrong decision in regard to a new job.

Rounds 1-5: Standard Format Statements to relieve body-centered doubt, stress, anger, tension, and fear in turn. She felt much better, more quiet, and she could stop the tears. She said she now had no doubt about the decision to take the new job.

In addition, she told the therapist that she could move her left foot as well, which she could not do before the session because she had a bunion operation one week ago. The therapist wrote, "Sometimes it is very funny what will happen during Dynamind."

Case F12404-Fear of love: A man of forty-seven had a problem receiving love from other people. He always felt doubt inside when he recognized that someone liked him. He felt this not only with new acquaintances, but with his wife and four children. He had a hard childhood and believed that he always had to be good and perfect. Because of this he was also hypercritical of others. Now he was very sad that he could not enjoy the real love of his wife.

First, the therapist guided him through several rounds of Dynamind for the general relief of stress, fear, doubt, anger, and tension. Then he was guided through two minutes of rounds using Blanket Forgiveness for his parents. When that was finished he had a smile on his face. Then the more specific rounds began.

Round 1: "There is doubt in my body and my mind when I feel love from another person…" He felt much better.

Round 2: A Power Statement for "I have no doubt when I feel loved!"

Round 3: Blanket Forgiveness for his wife. He felt good.

Round 4: A Power Statement for "I can enjoy the good feelings of love from my wife and other people." He said this strongly and felt so good that tears were running over his face and he smiled freely. He had been going twice a week to a psychotherapist for twelve years without any result like this.

Case F69605-Fear of not getting a job: A man of fifty lost his job and had not received answers to any of the sixty applications he mailed out. This had produced a great deal of tension and fear, plus a strong sense of pressure in his stomach at level 7.

Round 1: "When I think about having lost my job I feel a strong pressure in my stomach…" Level 4. The client said, "Now I'm feeling more free and I can breathe much better.

Round 2: The same. Level 2.

The therapist then suggested an image and an affirmation of positive expectation for a new job that the man could use when he sent out a new application.

Five days later the man phoned, very excited, to say that he had an interview, and that the pressure in his stomach was gone. The therapist reminded him to use Dynamind for any unpleasant symptoms and gave him another positive image and affirmation.

Although the client was one of the final candidates for the job he did not get it. Nevertheless, he was quite certain of getting a job soon because "I'm using the Dynamind Technique every day and it helps me very much, along with the other techniques, to give me a feeling of inner power."

Case F69606-Fear of making up: A man of thirty-five broke up with his girlfriend, but lacked the confidence to make up with her even though she meant a lot to him. He was afraid that their relationship was finished. At the time of the session the fear of reaching out to her by phone or letter was level 10.

Round 1: "When I think about my girlfriend, I'm afraid the relationship is finished..." The client moved his shoulders and said he was feeling lighter, but the fear was still there at level 7.

Round 2: "Dear (girlfriend), I'm folding my hands together and I'm thinking about you, I'm loving you, please forgive me for being afraid that I'm losing you. Both of us want to see each other again, please make it happen, make it so." The man was smiling and feeling much lighter and more relaxed.

Round 3: The same. "The fear is gone, now I've such a good feeling and I'm having so much energy, that I'll call her right today."

Feedback after a couple of days: "We met together and

it was a wonderful evening. By the Dynamind Technique I've become less rough and more positive in certain situations."

Case F81807-Fear of calling: A woman was afraid of calling a person who previously had sent a complaining letter to the management of the company. She had been putting this task aside for several days. The intensity level of that fear was 5 initially.

Round 1: "Whenever I think of this person I'm afraid to call him…" After the first round the fear dropped to 3.

Round 2: "I'm still a little bit afraid of calling this person…" After this second round the fear was at 1, which the therapist believed to be a reasonable amount of excitement ahead of such a phone call, and they left it there.

The result was that she picked up the phone immediately and called the customer. It turned out to be quite a pleasant call, with a nice person at the other end.

Case F25808-Procrastination: This case involved a woman client who had a business newsletter to prepare, but she was procrastinating because of anxiety. This was causing problems between her and her life partner as well. Although the problem sounds simple, it took an hour to resolve because of the many layers involved.

Round 1: "I feel anxiety when I think about doing the newsletter…" This lessened the anxiety somewhat, so the next step was to locate the anxiety in a particular place.

Round 2: "I feel anxiety in my gut when I think about doing the newsletter…" That symptom went away and then she felt a pain in the back of her head.

Round 3: "I feel a pain in the back of my head when I think about doing the newsletter…" That cleared, and she felt pressure in her eyes.

Round 4: SFS for pressure in the eyes. That cleared and a few more similar rounds were done until the client was feeling neither anxiety nor other physical symptoms. It appeared as if the problem had been resolved, but when the therapist asked the client to picture herself actually doing the newsletter she rather quickly began to cry and whispered that when she thought about going home to face her partner, who at the moment was angry at her, she felt shame.

Several rounds were done to clear shame in different parts of her body, and this led to an admission of feeling generally unworthy, with the feeling located again in her gut. That was cleared, and led to work with several layers of physical pain. Once the pain was gone there appeared several layers of a curious need for the client to "isolate myself in my legs," which were also cleared. Then they returned to the newsletter issue.

By this time the client felt generally better about doing the newsletter, but overwhelmed by all the paper in her office that she had collected as material to put into it, and she wanted to get rid of it. A round was done for the power to get rid of the excess paper in her office, then some rounds for more physical pain that appeared, and the session finally ended with a series of Power Statements to be able to finish the newsletter. The client reported feeling much more confident, much calmer, and much lighter than when she had arrived.

Feedback: The client called a few days later to say that the Dynamind Technique allowed her to get started on the newsletter. She added that it was a very valuable technique and that she and her life partner were continuing to use it for all sorts of things.

Case F25809-Fear of observation: A woman client was anxious about being observed during the coming weekend for accreditation in a healing technique that she was learning.

Round 1: "When I think about my being observed this weekend I feel queasy…" That cleared and she said she felt calm. The therapist asked her to think again about the weekend and a new feeling arose.

Round 2: "When I think about my being observed this weekend, I'm afraid of being stupid…" She said the feeling changed and she now felt fear in her pelvis.

Round 3: SFS for the fear in her pelvic area. The feeling changed to numbness.

Round 4: SFS for numbness in her pelvic area. That cleared and she said she felt calm, surprisingly calm.

The therapist asked her to think again about the weekend, and she said she had trouble focusing on it.

The session ended with a Power Statement for confidence and the client stated that she felt much better, much calmer and more confident, "just great."

Case F41910-Stuttering: The client was a woman in her fifties with a history of severe emotional, physical, and sexual abuse. She was also in constant pain from fibromyalgia. The therapist had sent her to a pain management group but the woman became very anxious about being around a lot of people and so upset that she could not sleep for a few nights. This was a few weeks before the session. She told the therapist that she had been in bed all day a few days ago and that she thought it was because she was still upset about the group and letting the therapist down. The therapist explained to her that the other therapist had said it was fine if the client did not want to join the group. When the current therapist asked the client to say that she understood that the other therapist was okay with her decision, the client could not say the words without strong stuttering. Then the Dynamind session began.

Round 1: "When I think about the (other) therapist I begin to stutter and that can change…" The client repeated the statement about the therapist, and although she was still stuttering, she was able to say all the words.

Round 2: The same Statement, followed by a Power Statement for confidence in speaking. The stuttering became less.

Round 3: The same SFS, plus a Symkey for the stuttering. The client was surprised at the request, but came up with a round, purple shape weighing a hundred pounds, and an angel to take it away. The client immediately said that her headache went away (this had been worked on before without success). After this round the client was able to complete the statement about the other therapist with minimal stuttering.

Case F13111-Lack of confidence: This client was a skilled psychotherapist, registered nurse, and Emergency Medical Technician in her early fifties who was also highly intuitive. However, her emotional problems from an abusive childhood had kept her from being able to work or live effectively for more than short periods of time. Level 6.

Round 1: "I've been doubting myself and acting unlovingly to myself, and that can change. I want to let my light shine and be secure—which includes feeling confident, loving myself, and having a sense of poise—and competent in the areas that have been a challenge for me." After the first round, she came down to a level 3, and said, "It feels warm and cozy," which was quite a remarkable shift for her. She also heard/felt in her mind the words, "You've been here all the time!" and "I'm here, it's OK." These inner statements were very meaningful to her.

After the second round with the same Statement, she came down to a 1, and said, "There is a definite energy shift in my body."

According to the therapist. "This speed and ease of change was quite remarkable for her, because her pattern has been that everything takes a lot of work and a lot of time and a lot of pain."

Case F13112-Performance anxiety: The client was a man who was anxious about his involvement and performance at an upcoming event, partly because he had never been to such an event, and partly because he was expected to lead a part of it. Anxiety level was 6-7, and he expressed a desire to "keep a little anxiety so I'll be able to keep that edge."

After the first round using an SFS for anxiety, he was at a 5. After the second round, he was at a 2. After the third round, he was at a 1, and that was fine with him, because he wanted to "keep that edge." He made several comments about the energies he felt moving in him during the Dynamind process, and that he was impressed with the results of the process.

Case FX13-Performance anxiety: "An older woman in her fifties was afraid of the on-the-job training we were about to start. Her fear disappeared completely after one round of Dynamind, with no visible signs of stress any more. She even agreed that one of her colleagues should be allowed to listen to the phone calls she would make."

Case FX14-Performance anxiety: "I was about to start training a woman of about thirty for telephone work. She stated that she had a lot of stress imagining that I would listen to the phone calls she would make. I asked her if she would be willing to do a little experiment that could help. She agreed, but she looked afraid, with eyes wide open and red spots appearing at her face and on her neck.

"Her stress level initially was at 8. It came down to 5 after the first round and 0 after the second. She looked at me with surprise and said: "Is this possible?" She had no red spots anymore and we had a very constructive training."

Phobias

A phobia is usually defined as an irrational fear,

having no basis in reality. I do not agree. Phobias are learned behaviors in response to a very unpleasant experience with a person, object, or activity. Just because someone observing the phobic behavior does not understand it, that does not make it irrational. Impractical, perhaps; unnecessary, yes; but irrational?

When I was very young I had a dog phobia which didn't make sense to anyone, including me, until I learned that as a baby I had been badly scratched on the face by a puppy. My sister's spider phobia would seem all out of proportion to any current encounter with a spider, except for the knowledge that she had learned how to react to spiders with strong emotion from our mother. I have no idea why my youngest son was afraid of the ocean, but I trust that his subconscious mind had a very good reason for it. A person with a phobia is experiencing a very real fear which needs to be respected. Fortunately, Dynamind is a very real technique that can help a person to unlearn it.

Case F71215-Fear of thunder: The client was a child of twelve with a lifelong terror of thunderstorms.

Round 1: SFS for the fear of thunderstorms. The child reported a sensation of warmth in her hands that she did not like.

Round 2: SFS for the sensation of warmth. "The warmth is leaving my hands and I feel okay." After these two rounds her lifelong terror of thunderstorms was gone.

In a follow-up report her mother said that the girl had always been terrified of loud noises, especially thunderstorms. She would go into a state of terror that was hard to deal with because there was no talking to her, and she wouldn't hear you anyway. At the very first sign of a storm she would be in the basement, hiding, where she couldn't hear the noise. This had been going on her whole life and the mother had tried, in her words, "Everything!"

After the Dynamind session there were a few small storms in the area, and the girl did not react to them. When the mother asked her why not, the girl said that "they were just little ones." Previously she would have been down in the basement at the very first small rumble. Then, when a good-sized thunderstorm occured, the girl called down from her bedroom and asked, "Mom, was that a big storm?" The mother said it was, but the girl didn't think it was very big. Later on there were a series of storms that the mother described as "whoppers, right on top of us, and they didn't even faze her!!! Even I was scared today, and I love a good storm! On behalf of my daughter I say, thank you, thank you, thank you!"

Case F71216-Fear of the dark: A young boy with a fear of being alone in the dark.

Round 1: "I have a problem with feeling afraid to be in my room alone…" The boy fell asleep immediately and the problem did not return.

Case F12417-Fear of loss: A woman of forty-two with fears of losing everything important to her. Level 9.

Round 1: "I have doubt in my body…" Level 5.

Round 2: "I still have doubt in my body and my brain…" Level 0.

Round 3: "I have fear in my body…" After a deep Breath she was smiling, and everything was okay.

Case F12418-Fear of descending: A woman of forty with a fear of walking downhill. Level 10.

Round 1: "I have fear in my body…" Level 5.

Round 2: "When I think about walking down a hill or a mountain, I feel fear in my chest…" Level 2. She became aware of anger toward her husband.

Round 3: "When I think of my husband wanting me to walk down a hill or a mountain, I feel anger in my body…" Level 1. Now she felt doubt that she could really get rid of the fear.

Round 4: "There is doubt in my body when I think about walking down a hill…" Level 0.

The therapist asked her if she could imagine walking down a hill or a mountain and she said, "Yes, I can do it." Before the session she had big red spots on her face, and afterward they were gone.

Case F81819-Fear of driving: A woman of thirty-six was afraid of driving in a big city. She said that she would lose her concentration because of so much information and that would make her become frightened. The intensity of the fear was level 7.

Round 1: "When I think of driving in a big city, I feel fear…" She then suddenly felt pain in her stomach.

Round 2 worked with this pain, and she felt a stiff neck after it.

Round 3 cleared the neck stiffness, and this was replaced by pain in the knees. After round 4 for the knee pain she suddenly felt relaxed, had no more pain at all, and smiled at the therapist. She said that the fear still was at level 4, but she felt much better about going to town.

Case F41920-Social phobia: The client came in feeling extremely anxious because she might have to go to a party in three weeks. One of the symptoms was a nervous stomach at level 10.

Round 1: "When I think about going to the party I feel nervous in my stomach…" Level down to 5.

Round 2: Same SFS. Level 4.

Round 3: Same SFS plus a Power Statment for confidence. No change. The therapist had the client do a form of piko-piko breathing while saying "relax" to herself. After a few breaths she felt much better about the party, but got a headache.

Round 4: SFS for the headache. No change. The

therapist asked the client what she thought was stopping her from relaxing and she said that she kept thinking about the party. The therapist had the client focus on her feet for a minute, then do more piko-piko breathing.

Round 5: SFS for the headache. All of the symptoms were gone.

Case F35321-Fear of illness: The client was a woman of twenty with an infection in in her leg that had been recurring for about a year. The presenting problem was that every time she thought of the infection she felt a lot of fear in her heart and throat, and tears came to her eyes. The level of fear before the session was 8.

Round 1: "I have a feeling of fear in my heart..." Level 5. She felt a little more happy.

Round 2: "I have a feeling of fear in my throat..." Level 2. She said that she felt even better, and there were no more tears. She no longer felt that the infection was a problem, but something else instead. She also reported the appearance of another symptom.

Round 3: "When I think of my infection I feel pressure in my solar plexus..." Felt improvement, and a little dizziness.

Round 4: A Symkey was used of writing the word, "infection," on a dry erase board, and then erasing it. This brought complete relief and smiles.

Case F35322-Mistrust of men: The client was a woman in her twenties with a difficulty in trusting men. She rated the level at 10.

Round 1: "I have feelings of not trusting men..." This brought out an awareness of how she judged men, and the fact that she did not like how they "ogled" women.

Round 2: "I have feelings of judgment of men who ogle women. Level 7. Then the client changed the problem to one of not feeling that she was beautiful enough.

Round 3: An SFS was done for this problem, along with a Symkey of her as a beautiful, sexy woman. Level 6. She admitted then that she wanted the man she was with to ogle her and not other women.

Round 4: "I have a feeling of lack of confidence in my beauty and this can change. I want to be as confident and beautiful as a jaguar." Level 3.

The session ended with a Dynamind Toner and Developer. There was a dramatic change in the client's appearance. She glowed and smiled. She said she loved this technique because it was quick and didn't involve years of therapy which she has experienced in the past. She went out to practice this with other issues.

Case F35123-Fear of dreams: The client was a woman in her thirties with fears related to dreams of the Holocaust. The intensity level was 8.

Round 1: "I have a feeling of not being able to breathe..." The feeling was slightly better.

Round 2: "I have discomfort in my lungs..." Intensity level moved to zero for the breathing difficulty. However, the fear feelings were still intense, and centered around fears of survival, potential threats against her life, and expectations of being tortured and killed.

Round 3: "I have feelings of fear..." A Symkey was used that began with an image of drowning and darkness, and ended with being enveloped in the love of God.

Round 4: "I have feelings of being tortured and killed..." The Symkey for this round was a dungeon changed into a dove. The intensity level of the fears went down to 2.

Panic

Named after a Greek god of the forest whose followers supposedly engaged in ritual chaotic behavior, panic refers to an extreme degree of fear that, today, ranges from wild emotional outbursts at one end, to frozen helplessness at the other end.

Case F12424-Panic attacks: A woman of thirty-nine with fears about life, pain and tension in the breast, and panic attacks for the past thirteen years. Tension and pain in the breast were placed at level 6.

To begin, this therapist likes to do what she calls a complete Clearing, which means several rounds of Dynamind for the general relief of stress, fear, doubt, anger, and tension. Then she had the client work on specific symptoms.

Round 1: "There is pain and tension in my breast…" Level 4.

Round 2: "There is fear in my breast…" Level 0.

During the Breath segment the client got a severe panic attack, like an angina pectoris attack, and the therapist moved her immediately into five minutes of rounds using Blanket Forgiveness for her family. She was much better then, so the therapist had her do Dynamind with the Power Statements: "My body has the power to live without fear…" and "I have the power to live without fear…"

At the end of those rounds the client turned around and hugged the therapist "very strong and long." Tears were running down the client's face and she said, "I feel better thank you, all the bad thinking in my head is gone."

A final note from the therapist: "What a wonderful job." (SK comment: Please note how effective forgiveness was at stopping the panic attack.)

Case F12425-Panic: A young lady of sixteen who had difficulty breathing at night, and would wake up every hour with panic attacks. Level 8.

Round 1: "There is a feeling of fear in some parts of my body…" Level 3.

Round 2: "There is still fear in some parts of my

body…" No change.

The girl told the therapist about the problems with her parents because of a divorce, and so the therapist took her through a third round of Blanket Forgiveness, which brought the panic problem down to level 2. For the fourth round she did the forgiveness Statement again and added an image of giving flower leis to the parents and the problem level went to 0.

Case F69626-Terror: A woman of fifty-two was in a course to develop her psychic skills when she became overwhelmed with memories of how her grandmother terrorized her when she had to live with her during most of her teenage years. These memories were so strong that she could not banish them. At the time of the session she gave them a level 9 intensity.

Round 1: "I feel a strong fear and terror when I think of the time with my grandmother…" She felt a bit better. The level was 7.

Round 2: The same. Level 4.

Round 3: The same. Level 1-2. She was feeling much better now and the therapist reminded her to use Dynamind if the fears came up again.

Feedback after two weeks: "She is feeling well since the day we've done the exercises. Even when she is thinking of the time with her grandmother, she doesn't feel the fear and the terror any more. She can just think about it without any negative feeling."

Case F25827-Nightmares: Although the setting was very informal, the situation was handled like a regular session. While at home, the therapist's daughter awoke with a panic attack, having had nightmares frequently throughout the night. First the therapist guided her daughter through a technique for rewriting the nightmares, and then they went on to Dynamind. The intensity level of the panic feeling was then at level 8.

Round 1: "I have tension throughout my body and this can change…" Level 2.

Round 2: The same. The feeling of tension disappeared.

Round 3: "I have panic inside my body…" It lessened.

Round 4: The same. The sensation then went to a feeling of panic in her chest.

Round 5: "I have panic inside my chest…" She felt relaxed and sleepy.

Round 6: A Power Statement for feeling confident, relaxed and competent was "tapped in," and the girl was 100% better.

Miscellaneous Fears

Cases which are difficult to classify, or of which I have only a few cases to share at this time, are listed here.

Case F25828-General anxiety: A woman client was experiencing anxiety around her job. She located it in her stomach.

Round 1: "I have anxiety in my stomach…" She said it significantly diminished, but was still there. The therapist asked her if she could come up with an image of what the anxiety felt like, and she described it as spinning blades. Then the therapist asked if she liked angels. The client smiled and said, "Very much."

Round 2: "I have blades spinning in my stomach and this can change. An angel takes the blades out of my stomach and takes them far far away." She reported that the pain was gone.

Case F25829-Hopelessness: A woman client was complaining about a feeling of hopelessness regarding her current circumstances. The therapist asked her if she experienced the hopelessness in a particular place in her body. First she said shoulders, then lungs, then settled on tightness in her throat. She was, in fact, barely able to talk and she sounded very constricted.

Round 1: "When I think about my life circumstances I feel tightness in my throat…" She said that it was better, but she still felt something there.

Round 2: "I feel fear in my throat when I think about my life circumstances…" It cleared, but she started coughing and began talking somewhat more freely. The therapist asked her to again think of her situation and she said she felt discouraged, with the feeling located in her chest.

Round 3: SFS for discouragement in her chest, and that cleared. Asked to think again about her situation, she replied that she wanted to feel numb and that that was in her sacrum (She also was having back problems.)

Round 4: "I want to feel numb in my lower back when I think about my life situation…" The pain in her back lessened significantly. Asked again about her situation she said she felt an overall tiredness.

Round 5: SFS for the feeling of tiredness. At that point she said she felt like the emotional charge had disappeared, although she still appeared quite subdued. This was followed by some symbol work without using Dynamind, and when she left she was feeling much more hopeful and talking freely.

Case F69230-Fear of self: A woman in her mid-thirties was working with ex-prisoners and had developed great fear after reading the case study of a murderer. The intensity of the fear was level 7.

Round 1: "When I think of this story in my files, I experience the most strange feelings…" No change.

Round 2: "I feel fear inside myself…" No change.

Round 3: "I have fear I could do something stupid…

" No change.

Round 4: "I have fear that I could kill someone myself..." Level 6.

Round 5: "I mistrust myself and that can change. I want that mistrust to go away, and I want to have total trust in myself!" This same Statement was used for three more rounds and at the end the feeling was at level 1.

Case F35131-Multiple fears: The client was a man in his thirties with many fears, strong opinions about many things, and a great need to assert his independence. The latter trait was evidenced in the session by his attitude toward the Dynamind format. Although the presenting problem was a fear related to an undisclosed childhood issue, the session included fears of intimacy, a sense of disconnectedness, and issues around his own intolerance of other people. Symkeys that were used involved energy blocks, feelings of constriction, shark attacks, war gods fighting, and changing of energy patterns by color, shape, texture and movement until they felt right to him.

In the words of the therapist, "He does not like to be told a set pattern that he has to follow, so he went on to change the ritual. He did not always use the tapping but did as the issue became deeper. He changed most of the words but continued to use the phrases " I have the feeling of" "and this will change." He often stated what will change and then what it will be changed into. He moved his body with jerks as he felt the energy patterns changing. He made physical movement patterns of letting go and bringing in. Sometimes he added sounds.

"The session was dramatic, with discussion of what he did not tolerate in other people. He used word play, analytical patterns of thought, dramatization of movement and sound as he worked with changing energy patterns. He would not use the rating scale, but said that he felt better and

173

the next day said that he felt the continuing effects.

Feedback from days later: "He continues to say he is working on the Dynamind Technique and feels its continuing effects but does not use the ritual of words and tapping. He likes to work with self talk and energy patterns."

Case F35132-Fearful expectations: A woman in her fifties had strong fear when she did not hear from her daughter when she expected to. Level 8.

Round 1: SFS for the feeling of fear. Level 6.

Round 2: same statement. Inserted a Symkey of replaying the scenario of bad things happening to her daughter and changing the scenario to good things instead. Level 4.

Round 3: same statement. Inserted a Symkey which started with a threatening dragon breathing fire. This was changed to meeting the dragon, retreating, going forward and jumping over him. The dragon was still behind and following, so she kept going down the path to a pool of rainbow-colored water and a tree with a switch in it. She pulled the switch and the rainbow colors arched to the dragon and turned him into Puff, a friendly dragon. The session ended at Level 2.

Case FX33-Obsessive thinking: "I've been using this wonderful technique to stop my obsessive thinking patterns; heal old emotional wounds; to go to sleep quickly instead of reading for an hour or two; to work on chronic and acute aches and pains; and to help the family with physical problems; but the greatest of these (at this moment) is to be able to stop my obsessive thinking!! I've been released from bondage!!"

Chapter Seven
DISTANT DYNAMIND

In my Dynamind workshops I teach several methods to do what I call "Distant Dynamind." The most ordinary method, which has been described already in some cases, is to guide someone through the Dynamind Technique by telephone. Since the usual way to help someone is to guide them through it anyway, this is no more than an extended version of the same thing and it works just as well.

Even though all the cases presented in this book so far involve the use of Dynamind with spoken words and physical touch by the person doing the process, I did mention in Chapter Two that you can do the process mentally. And I described how you can do Dynamind for someone else, if the other person is not able to do it for any reason. Two more ways of doing Dynamind can be thought of as extensions of these two variations.

The first way consists of thinking about the person you want to help, whether that person is present or far away, and then doing Dynamind on yourself for the other person's benefit. A Statement for this way would take the form "John has a problem and that can change. I want the problem to go away," or "John wants the problem to go away." And then you would tap yourself and breathe. As an alternative, you could do the whole thing mentally.

The second way is only suitable for people with a fair degree of self confidence. In this way of doing Dynamind you imagine that you are the other person, with the other person's problem, and then you do Dynamind on yourself, mentally or physically, as the other person, and use your own body as feedback for whether there has been a change or not. At the end of such a session you imagine you are you again.

Now, if you want a scientific explanation for how this could possibly be effective, you are not going to get one. It doesn't matter to me whether it is understandable or not, the results speak for themselves. If you wish to interpret the results as coincidence, that's fine with me. If you wish to interpret the results as evidence of telepathy, that's fine, too. Personally, I don't believe in coincidence and, because of my shamanic training, I don't believe in telepathy, either—I just assume it. The cases will be presented as they were reported, without any attempt to justify them.

Some of our Dynamind Practitioners specialize in Distant Dynamind, and others use it sporadically. Regardless, all would agree that good results are very dependent on good focus. Many of the cases presented will be in the form of anecdotes.

The first section will describe cases in which the Dynamind Technique was used as a mental adjunct to a different, very physical and formal type of therapy.

The second section describes cases where the mental form of Dynamind was primary, but supported by another type of touch therapy.

The third section will present a few miscellaneous cases which did not involve any direct contact with the client or subject, and the fourth section will list some interesting cases in which personal change apparently influenced the behavior of other people related to the problem.

The fifth section will cover most of the cases we have on file of using Distant Dynamind with animals.

The seventh and last section is extremely speculative,

as it involves the use of Distant Dynamind in more unusual circumstances and for more unusual purposes which may or may not influence the way we think about reality.

Using Distant Dynamind To Assist Another Form Of Therapy

Comment from the therapist: "Please understand that with all treatments reported I am applying the Dynamind Technique mentally in conjunction with my usual physical therapy. This means that I am putting my hands on the patients and from this moment on, after having made mental contact with and having received the blessing and the help from what some people call God, Buddha, Christ, Zen, Tao, Mickey Mouse or Pinocchio, I start the physical treatement and the Dynamind. You asked me whether I actually feel that Dynamind is contributing significantly to my treatments, and I have to say that there is absolutely no doubt. I could never obtain such results without the Dynamind Technique."

Case T13301-Pain in the head: The client was a man with pain in his head after a fall. The pain had persisted for six weeks and was at level 7 at the time of the session. Several rounds with SFSs for the pain were done and at the end the pain was gone.

Case T13302-Upper back pain: The client was a woman with extremely strong pain at a point between her shoulders, recurring over several years. Intensity level was 9. She had just come from another therapist whose treatment had increased the pain.

Three rounds of Dynamind using SFSs for the pain during a fifteen-minute treatment brought the intensity down to 2.

Case T13303-Lower back pain: The client was a woman with pain in the lower part of her back that she had had for five years. It was at level 8 at the time of the session.

During treatment three rounds of Dynamind were done for pain, anger, and fear. At the end of the treatment the pain was down to level 1.

Case T13304-Depression: A woman client had been experiencing depression for six months. The SFS used was "I feel lost and depressed..." After five treatments she felt far better, her morale went up, and she had some sunny days again.

Case T13305-Multiple symptoms: A woman had fallen into an air supply tube a distance of approximately four meters (about thirteen feet). As a result of this accident her spine received a shock and in addition to enormous back pain, she suffered from headache, she felt dizzy, and she could not lift up her right arm. This had been a problem for three years, and the overall intensity level at the time of the first session was 9.

Mental SFS during Treatment 1: "I cannot lift my right arm..."

Mental SFS during Treatment 2: "I have a terrible headache on my right side..."

Mental SFS during Treatment 3: "I am still getting very dizzy..."

Mental SFS during Treatment 4: "My whole back is blocked..."

After four treatments she called the therapist and told him she would not need any more treatment because she was feeling great.

Case T13306-Pregnancy: A woman had one child and wanted another, but she had not been able to get pregnant for a whole year. No intensity scale was used, but she was nervous, tense, and bad-tempered.

The mental SFS used during each treatment was "My problem is that I can not get pregnant any more..." After ten treatments she got pregnant.

Using Distant Dynamind With The Support Of Another Therapy

Comment regarding the therapist: This therapist has had considerable professional experience as a health practitioner and she has developed her own unique way of applying Distant Dynamind. Typically, she makes physical contact with the client to establish rapport. This contact is often in the form of a tension-releasing technique called "Kahi," which is described in my book, *Urban Shaman*. She uses it by placing one hand on the client's chest and the other on the client's back and then she lets her attention flow between her hands as she breathes deeply. When the situation allows it, she also likes to do something she calls a "Complete Clearing," which is a variation of the Dynamind Toner described earlier. With the client thus prepared, she begins the mental Dynamind for the specific problems.

Case T12407-Shoulder pain: "I met a woman of eighty in a shop in my little village, she had a big pain in her left shoulder. I asked her if I could help her, and she said it was okay. Then I started Dynamind the mental way. I did the Statement for her, as well as the Touch and the Breath. In the moment when I put my hands around her shoulder to make the Statement, she told me that the pain was less, and after doing Dynamind the pain was gone, and she could move her shoulder and her arm. She looked at me and had tears in her eyes, because the doctor told her that he couldn't help her because she is too old and the bones are sick."

Case T12408-Foot pain: "A woman of sixty-three came to me with pain in the left and the right foot, because she was in Rome to see the Pope and she was walking for four days to see the city! She could not move well, but she was wearing good shoes.

I did the Dynamind mentally two times for the pain

in her feet, and after that she got up and had no more pain. Next day she gave me a call to tell me that the pain was still gone."

Case T12409-Autistic child: (SK note: According to the Autism Society of America, "Autism is a complex developmental disability that typically appears during the first three years of life. The result of a neurological disorder that affects the functioning of the brain, autism and its associated behaviors have been estimated to occur in as many as 2 to 6 in 1,000 individuals (Centers for Disease Control and Prevention 2001). Autism is four times more prevalent in boys than girls and knows no racial, ethnic, or social boundaries. Family income, lifestyle, and educational levels do not affect the chance of autism's occurrence." Conventional treatment is designed individually, and may include speech therapy, social skill development, the use of medication, sensory integration and dietary changes.)

"A five-year-old boy was diagnosed by doctors as being hyperactive and autistic, and they only thing they could offer was a special gym and ergotherapy, the treatment of disease by muscular exercise. His mother told me he had been like this since he was two when she fell down some stairs with the boy in her arms. She had broken her foot and there was nothing physically wrong with the boy, but after the accident he didn't want to speak any more, and would only say a few words like a two-year-old might do. She told me that when she looked in his eyes after the accident they were full of fear. The boy spent a lot of time in front of the television, and he only spoke words from children's movies. He also did not like to be touched.

I asked him if I could touch him and tap on his chest. He came to me and I did the mental way of Dynamind first with fear in his body, then anger in his body. I held him with my hands on his chest and on his back. He took a very deep breath and he started burping very often and very loud. Then I made some Statements with 'When he thinks about the accident he feels fear in his body…' and 'There is fear in his neck…' After this I did a Power Statement: 'His body has the power to pronounce the words normally…" After all this I prayed for him with my hands on his back and chest and did the Breath.

Then he had to go to the toilet a lot to urinate (10 times in one hour) and he burped very often. Finally, he came to me, layed in my arms, and said to me: 'Nice lady do tapping to me!'

His mother was so happy and she told me that he never did this before and she could feel that he had very hot hands and feet, and his face was red and warm and he got more quiet."

Case T12410-Shoulder pain: "A truck driver of forty-seven had pain in his right shoulder for ten years. The doctor said he could not do anything because it came from shifting the gears in the truck. I asked him if I could touch him, and he said yes, so I put my hands on his chest and his back and then I did the mental way of Dynamind with a Statement for the pain in his right shoulder. I did this twice and the pain was gone. He gave me a kiss and said, 'Thank you, Little Witch.'"

Case T12411-Head pain: "A man of sixty-seven had strong pain on the right side of his head all the way to his right shoulder, and it was so severe that he could not even touch the hairs on his head in that area. He had had this problem for ten years and no one could help him. He gave the pain a level 8. I did Dynamind the mental way while holding my hands on his chest and back.

Round 1: 'This man has a pain on the right side of his head…' Level 7.

Round 2: 'This man has anger under the skin of his

181

head on the right side…' Level 3.

Round 3: 'This man still has anger under the skin of his head on the right side…' Level 1. After that he felt okay."

Case T12412-Neurodermatitis: "During dinner at a restaurant I saw a one-year-old boy at a neighboring table with red spots on his face and arms, and he was continually scratching these areas. After eating chips and ketchup it was getting worse. Finally I couldn't stand it any longer and I got up went over there and told the mother that I could try to do something with him which wouldn't hurt and wouldn't cost any money. She said it was okay to do something. I was right when I noticed that he had neurodermatitis, and I estimated it at level 9. Since it was a public situation I did Dynamind the mental way.

I held him in my arms, gave him a lot of Kahi, and he got more quiet.

Round 1: 'There is unspoken anger in some parts of this boy's body…'

Round 2: 'There is fear in some parts of this boy's body…'

I gave him Kahi to his face and to his arms and asked his body to change the pain. After 15 minutes the mother came to our table and said, 'Thank you for everything, he stopped the scratching and the red spots are completely gone.'"

Case T12413-Autistic boy: An autistic boy of thirteen was hurting himself and others, he could not speak, and his hands were bound along his body. His mother had had a lot emotional problems during pregnancy. The therapist did the mental form of Dynamind.

After the first round, using an SFS for anger, the boy looked at her and spoke very softly: "Anger, that can change."

This was followed by three rounds with fear, doubt,

and tension.

Then she used the Statement "When this child was an unborn baby he had the feeling that he was not welcome in his family, and this can change. He wants this feeling to go away."

This was followed by the Power Statement "This child has the power to pronounce every word clearly that he wants to speak, yes he does, make it happen."

The therapist did this on two different days during a week before the children of his school went on a supervised holiday. One of the teachers at the school told the therapist the the boy she had worked with "spoke like a waterfall" during the holiday, and that every day he was speaking more clearly and behaving better.

From the therapist: "I do therapy two days a week at this school for disadvantaged children, and each time I see this boy he comes us to me and says, 'Grateful.' I say 'For what?' And he says, 'You.' Thank God for Dynamind."

Case T12414-Allergy: "A man of forty-two was allergic to flowers and grasses and during a party he started to sneeze, his eyes teared, and his voice went flat. I did mental Dynamind for him, first for anger, and then for the sensation he had like a feather tickling his nose and his eyes. He felt much better, and three months later he still had had no more allergy symptoms. When I saw him recently he said that he doesn't believe in what I do, but the allergy is still gone and he is very happy about that. I find it interesting that he refuses to believe in spite of the results. For me, it just means that Dynamind can work with or without belief."

Case T12415-Autistic adult: (SK note: This case involves Dynamind, but more than anything it demonstrates the value of love, compassion, and persistence in the healing process. The therapist changed the name of the client, and I have changed it again. The case history is rather long, but I think the details are important.)

"The Story of Bob, an autistic man of twenty.

Although Bob is autistic, he is a very nice person. Sometimes he is very hyperactive, and he also has epilepsy. His brain is like a camera and all the things he does he will do twice.

When I asked his mother about the past, she told me that he has been officially autistic since the age of six. Before that he was very slow in his growth and behavior. The mother had been sexually abused as a child, and she had relationship problems. Bob was raised by his grandmother, but he was hidden away because he was not normal. When he was two a woman in his neighborhood found him sitting in the middle of a street, with the cars driving right and left around him, and no one knows how long he was there. After this he was locked up in the house, sometimes in a dark room, so he slept the whole day.

When I met him the first day he looked very deep into my eyes, as if he wanted to look into my soul. At first his gaze was very strong, but after about two minutes he started to smile .

I began my therapy with Bob by doing ten minutes of Kahi on his chest and back. And then I did mental Dynamind. Bob was laying in my arms, and a friend of his said that Bob never did that before with strangers.

I made Statements about feelings of fear about being hidden away and other fears I thought he must have had, and more Statements to clear away anger, doubt, tension, and stress. I ended with some Power Statements about his ability to speak clearly. He was very quiet and smiling, and with every Round he got quieter.

After two hours of Dynamind I did a one-hour Hawaiian-style massage only on his upper body, because he didn't want to take off his pants. I worked first on his back and he shouted like an animal because he had fear, so I did it very softly and with a lot of Aloha. After ten minutes he could enjoy it because he was so relaxed. Then I tried to turn him on his back, but he refused to turn over, shouting again with fear. I did the massage on his front with him sitting up, and after a while he laid down with fear, but he did lie down. After fifteen minutes he was relaxed.

The next day I came back and did the same mental Statements with Dynamind, plus one more for his fear of lying on his back. I also did the same Kahi, but he didn´t want to sit with me quietly. He was smiling and he kept looking at the place where the massage table had been the day before, and he was touching himself with his hand on his chest. So I got the massage table from my car and put it in the living room in the same place and Bob took off all his clothes in a couple of minutes and jumped on the table and laughed very loud. He enjoyed the massage, and after forty-five minutes he turned very fast onto his back and smiled.

After two hours of massage he got an epileptic attack. Everyone was shocked, and they blamed me. I told them to come and watch how this could be changed. I gave him Kahi on his head and did mental Dynamind for the tension in his body. During the Breath I asked his body to lessen the tension as fast as possible. After one minute the attack was over, but I noticed something very important. His eyes had been looking 'left and up' and I remembered from my studies of Kinesiology this was an indication that he was focusing on mental images. Because of the tension state of his body and his behavior, I surmised that he was seeing images that induced great fear, probably memory images.

After the attack was over and he was relaxed again he slept for four hours. The next day I called his mother and she said that he had changed into a different Bob. He was very relaxed, smiling all the time, and he was trying to speak.

This was an very fantastic thing in my life. I learned so much, and I thank God for this. I think Bob will speak in a couples of weeks, like some other autistic people did after two weeks of Dynamind. Sometimes they just need more time."

Non-contact Healing Cases

Case T69616-Healing a wife: A man of fifty had already been to this therapist for a Dynamind session, and this time he wanted to know if it would be possible to support the healing progress of his wife, who had gone through a big operation the day before.

The therapist told him it would be possible, but it would work best if his wife wanted the same thing. The man said that his wife was unhappy in the hospital and wanted to go home as quickly as soon as she could. The doctors said that after this kind of operation you usually had to remain in the hospital for one and a half to two weeks.

The therapist told the man that he could help his wife because everyone is connected, and that the more that his intention was filled with love, the better the results would be. The man was ready and willing and the therapist guided him through the process of Distant Dynamind.

The Statement was "My dearest wife, I'm putting my fingers together and I'm thinking about you. You're worried a bit, that you may be have to stay for a long time in the hospital, and that can be changed. Both of us are wishing that the doubt may disappear, and that soon we'll be together again. Please, make it happen, and it is so. Your operation has been successful, your self-healing energy is working optimally." Then the man tapped on his own body and did the Breath.

The therapist asked the man how he was feeling and he said, "I'm feeling very good and I've the feeling that the healing process will be good." The same process was repeated and the therapist told the man to repeat it as often as he wanted to.

Feedback about two weeks later: The healing process was so successful that his wife was able to go home after only one week.

Case T15217-Feeling faint: A bride in her twenties felt faint at the wedding reception and had to leave the room. She was gone for a half hour. The therapist did mental Dynamind on behalf of the subject.

Round 1: "I feel faint..." As soon as the round was over the bride came back and danced the rest of the evening without any adverse symptoms.

Case TX18-Headache: "My boyfriend called me from his office in another city to say that he had such a bad headache that he couldn't even make the Dynamind work. He asked me if I could do distant healing for him right then. We hung up and I did three rounds of standard Dynamind for him, one for the headache, one for stress in his head, and one for anger. After this I certainly felt better, so I called him back and he said that he felt better, too. Thirty minutes after that he called again to say that the pain was all gone."

Case TX19-Headache: "My grandson was having headaches during the day. I heard about it in the evening during a phone call with my daughter, his mother, when he was already sleeping. I advised her how to do Distant Dynamind in his place. Next day, he was alright. No pains anymore."

Case T55520-School: A little girl, age 4, didn't want to go to school. Her mother asked the therapist to do something for her. The therapist decided to try Distant Dynamind.

She made a connection by saying the name of the girl three times and imagining herself to be the little girl.

In her mind she looked through the eyes of the girl into the classroom to see if there could be anything wrong there, but she didn't sense anything wrong, so she started doing Dynamind.

She used the SFS "I like going to school, yes I do…" and while she was saying it she actually saw herself happily dancing to school in the way little girls sometimes do. She did the process three times and then said her own name three times, loud and clear, to get back to herself again.

The mother of the girl told the therapist a few days later that her daughter was going happily to school now. There was no problem in the morning putting on her coat and shoes, but when they came to the classroom she started to cry a little. This made the therapist realize that she had never pictured the girl going happily into the classroom. However, the problem of going into class solved itself within a week.

Case T71221-Forgetfulness: "My daughter, twelve, generally forgets to take her sandwich to school, which infuriates my husband, who prepares it specially for her in the morning. That morning she was about to leave, and the sandwich was still on the table. I quickly said to myself "My daughter generally forgets to take her sandwich to school and this can change. I want her to remember to take her sandwich now". At that very moment she turned round (as though she had heard me, although I did it mentally), went to the table and took it! And since then she has been taking it every day without anybody reminding her to do it!!"

Animal Influence

Case T12422-A German Shepherd dog: "My neighbor's six-year-old German Shepherd dog, Goldie, was barking and howling all day long and into the night. He was not allowed to stay in the house during the night, because he has his own little house outside. His owner was a very strong, loud old man. Sometimes Goldie would bite other dogs, sometimes not. Sometimes he would be very friendly, and sometimes he was really bad.

I thought that fear might be his problem, so I asked the owner, and he told me that Goldie had some kind of fear that made him unsure of himself.

So I did the mental form of Dynamind with: 'The dog Goldie has fear in his body…' and 'The dog Goldie has doubt in his body…'

When I started the tapping over the Thymus point of the dog, he became more quiet and he looked at me. After that session he is not yet completely healed, but we can sleep in the night without hearing his barking, except when the church bells are ringing."

Case T12423-A Persian cat: "Jerry, our thirteen-year-old Persian male cat, had a very strong personality, but he seemed to be very lonely, so we bought him a seven-week-old white Persian female cat to keep him company. Actually, she was really more for me than for him. I named her Spa, because she is like a spa for my soul. Jerry didn't like her because now he had to share our love with her, and he didn't want to do this. For four days he was sleeping downstairs without food, and when Spa approached him he was very agressive toward her. So I had to do something.

Round 1: 'There is anger in the body of my cat Jerry…'

Round 2: 'There is a feeling of fear in the body of my cat Jerry because he is afraid of not being loved…'

Round 3: 'The body of my cat Jerry has the power to accept and love the little kitten Spa…'

Round 4: 'My cat Jerry has the power to share our love with the kitten Spa…'

The next day he came up from downstairs and he

189

took a little bit of food. The next day after that he became more friendly toward her. Now they sleep and eat together, and it is so nice."

Case T12424-A Rottweiler: "Our butcher had an eight-year-old Rottweiler named Butch who was afraid of thunder and lightning. During such a storm he would always howl in his doghouse and his body would tremble all over. I decided to do Distant Dynamind for him.

Round 1: 'Butch has fear in his body…'

Round 2: 'Butch has a fear of thunder and lightning in his body…'

Round 3: Butch has the power to live without fear of thunder and Lightning…'

After three weeks the butcher told me that Butch doesn't howl any more during a thunderstorm. Now he only has a little shaking of his body."

Case T12425-A cow: "Josie was a cow who had problems walking because she had an inflammation in all her feet. I think she was full of anger because she is the smallest one in the herd, and all the other cows pushed her away during the feeding time. I did Distant Dynamind for her.

Round 1: 'There is anger in the body of the cow Josie…'

Round 2: 'The cow Josie has anger in all four feet…'

She could walk better after that, and she was a little bit faster, but we will see how much improvement she has in a couple more days."

Case T69626-Hunting dog: "I was sitting in my office next door and I couldn't concentrate because of the howling of a neighbor's dog, which sounded like a screaming child. I decided to do Distant Dynamind.

I thought of the dog and made the Statement 'Lobo is feeling alone and sad, that can be changed. I'm wishing that he will get more attention, please make it happen, and it is so.' Mentally I tapped him 7 times lightly on the middle of the chest (Thymus area), tapped 7 times on the left shoulder and 7 times on the right shoulder, and 7 times on the C7 vertebra. Then I did the Breath.

The howling sound was changing, it became more soft. It was rather a gentle barking now. I repeated the technique and in my thoughts I massaged his head and his back. Within five minutes he became calm. The biggest surprise for me was that when I came out of the house and called him, he wagged his tail, and when I came to the enclosure, he came to me and wanted me to massage his head and back. In the meantime, I'm able to relax Lobo by the Dynamind Technique and the mental massage in a few minutes."

Case T69627-A pair of Watchdogs: "The wonderful experience I had with Lobo, the dog, made me wonder if it would be possible to get such good results with other dogs by applying the Dynamind Technique.

When I'm doing my jogging circuit I have to pass a farm with two dangerous watchdogs who bark loudly at me, showing their teeth. So the next time when I went for a jogging tour, a few minutes before reaching the house I contacted the dogs mentally. In my mind I tapped them 7 times lightly on the middle of the chest, 7 times on the left shoulder and 7 times on the right shoulder, and 7 times on the C7 vertebra. Then in my mind I said to them: 'You are both the best watchdogs I've ever seen before. You're watching the house perfectly and your master must be very proud of you. I'm happy to see you, but you don't have any reason to frighten me and to show me your teeth every time I'm walking by. I'm just walking by your territory, please do respect it, and so it is.' Then I repeated the Dynamind Technique three times.

When I reached the farm both of the dogs were

standing at the entrance. They gave no sound and were just looking at me. I got goose flesh, not because of the dogs, but because of the effect of what I had just done."

Case TSK28-German Shepherd: Inspired by some of the above cases I decided to try this form of Distant Dynamind myself when I encountered an aggressively barking German Shepherd during a walk in a small town in the State of Michigan. First I imagined an energetic connection between us, then in my mind I said "Good boy, good job, your master must be proud of you, but you can relax now." Lastly I did the Touch and Breath, and as soon as I finished the Breath the dog stopped barking, sat down, and just looked at me calmly.

Case TSK29-Neighborhood dogs: Near the end of the same walk a loud noise in the area stimulated the barking of about half a dozen dogs in the neighborhood, none of which I could see. More out of curiosity than anything else I established my imagined connection with all of them and did the same Distant Dynamind process as above. Again, as soon as I finished they all stopped barking.

Cases For Speculation

Comment: These cases are unusual because they imply that our thoughts may affect our experience more than we normally suppose. In these cases the person doing the Distant Dynamind is trying to influence the external environment. These cases do not prove anything, of course, except how interesting human behavior is.

Case T71230-Attention: "We went to visit friends with my daughter. Our friend's daughter got into an endless telephone conversation in another room and my daughter felt left aside and rejected. I said to myself "My daughter's friend is not paying attention to her and this can change. I want her friend to pay attention to her," and as soon as I finished the Breath, she appeared! Then it happened again, and I did this again, and immediately the friend called my daughter to her room."

Case T69231-Fax machine: "A teacher was expecting a fax, but the machine refused to accept it. Over and over the call came in, but the fax machine wasn`t able to reply properly. Since he expected an urgent document to come, he got more and more nervous. Then he remembered Dynamind, which I had explained to him earlier.

His SFS was 'I have a problem with my fax and this can change. I want this problem to go away!' While he was doing so, the fax phone rang again, and this time the machine was able to process the document without any further technical intervention from his side."

Case TSKK32-A zipper: While guiding some people through a park on Kauai I had to use the restroom. When I tried to zip up my fly before coming back out, however, the zipper would not work no matter how I tugged and pulled and twisted it. Just before giving up and facing acute embarrassment I recalled a similar experience mentioned by one of the Practitioners, so with nothing to lose I did a Standard Statement for the stuck zipper and when I finished the zipper came up easily.

On the one hand I realize that this kind of experience could be considered trivial and silly, but on the other hand it could turn out to be significant if enough people discover that they can have a positive influence on and a rapid resolution of the multitude of small problems that come up in our daily lives. If nothing else, trying this on your own may lead to some interesting... coincidences...

Appendix
DYNAMIND PRACTITIONERS AND TEACHERS

If you would like to contact a Certified Dynamind Practitioner or Teacher, go to the web page listing at www.huna.org/html/dmtprac.html.

For becoming a Certified Dynamind Practitioner or Teacher you can use the information below.

Certification Procedure

Serge Kahili King, Ph.D. will certify practitioners and teachers of the Dynamind Technique (DMT) who fulfill the following requirements.

Practitioners

1. There are two alternate study pre-requisites: a) attend one Dynamind Workshop by Serge Kahili King or a certified Dynamind Teacher, read Dr. King's book, Instant Healing, and study the Dynamind Pages online; b) Take the "Instant Healing Home Study Course," available through The Huna Store online (www.huna.net).

2. Provide reports of 25 case studies (25 clients) using the format given below.

3. Pay a one-time $100 administrative/registration fee upon application for the Practitioner program. Payments can be made   online at www.huna.net/dmpay.html or by

check drawn on a U.S. bank and mailed to:
  Hunaworks, P.O. Box 223009, Princeville HI 96722 USA

  4. Application shall consist of a brief resume of pertinent experience, including current address, email and website, if any, and proof of having fulfilled the requirements.
  5. Email is the preferred format for reporting case studies, but typewritten reports will be accepted.

In return, Serge Kahili King will
  1. Provide comments on the case studies as they are submitted.
  2. Upon completion of the case study requirement, add the Practitioner's name and contact information to a Certified Dynamind Practitioner list as well as a Therapist List on the Huna Village (www.huna.org) website.
  3. Refer potential clients to the Practitioner as appropriate.
  4. Provide a forum for Practitioners to exchange information about the use of DMT.

Format for reporting case studies:
  1. Client: Sex and approximate age (child, adult, etc.).
  2. Problem: (what was the client's primary presenting problem? How long has it been a problem? What was the intensity level, if you used a scale?).
  3. Process: (describe what you did and what happened for each round). Include word or other variations used in each round. and any symbols used and the effects.
  4. Resolution: (describe the final result of the session or series of sessions).

Teachers

1. Follow Practitioner requirements 1-2.

2. Provide reports of 100 case studies (100 clients). The Practitioner cases may be included.

3. Take the Huna Teacher Training Home Study course available through The Huna Store online (www.huna.net), or provide evidence of teaching experience.

4. Pay a one-time $1000 administrative/registration fee upon applying for Teacher Certification, payable online at www.huna.net/dmpay.html or by mail to:

Hunaworks, P.O. Box 223009, Princeville HI 96722 USA

5. Follow the Guidelines for Dynamind Teachers, to be provided by Dr. King.

6. Provide personal contact information for communication and website use.

In return, Serge Kahili King will

1. Provide comments on the case studies as they are submitted.

2. Add the Teacher's name and contact information to a Certified Dynamind Teacher list on the Huna Village (www.huna.org) website with a link to the Teacher's website and schedule, if available.

2. Refer potential students to the Teacher as appropriate.

3. Provide updates on the practice and teaching of Dynamind as the information base grows.

Format for reporting case studies:

1. Follow the same format as for the Practioner program.